MW00620303

"I remember Sahara as a spring in the desert of the time!"

—Gloria Steinem

"I promise you will not put down this book. Leslie Cohen has the gift of being a wonderful writer with the added blessing of having a profoundly significant personal story to tell. It's one of those books whose time has come."

—Caroline Myss, author of *Intimate Conversations with the Divine* and *Anatomy of the Spirit*

"I love Leslie's book. It is beautifully written. The detail she gives is remarkable both about her relationship with Beth, the beginning of Sahara where I spent many an amazing evening, and even her days in Siena. Leslie brings it all back to life. Reading this book, I was brought back to the Upper East Side in the '70s. Leslie had a magnetic power, and it suffuses the pages of this book."

—Brenda Feigen, feminist activist, film producer, attorney, cofounder of *Ms. Magazine*, director with Ruth Bader Ginsburg of the ACLU's Women's Rights Project, and author of *Not One of the Boys: Living Life as a Feminist*

"Leslie's tribute to Sahara is testimony to the sanctuary we found in being together, feeling safe and enthralled by a sense of freedom. Whether you found that in the Duchess, Bonnie and Clyde's or the Cubbyhole, this is your invitation to revisit. Little compared with the sense of anticipation you felt walking through the door and into the glances, stares or smiles of women and that the next few hours held countless possibilities."

—Ginny Apuzzo, gay rights and AIDS activist; former executive director of the National LGBTQ Task Force; president of the New York State Civil Service Commission and commissioner of the New York State Department of Civil Service; and assistant to the president for Management and Administration for the Clinton Administration

"Sahara was the only female place that I felt comfortable as I identified with the atmosphere and the women who patronized it—fashionable, glamorous, and happy. I thank Leslie Cohen for her imagination and design for her creation. The only woman's club that I continue to hold in my memory."

—Patricia Field, Emmy Award–winning costume designer, stylist, and fashion designer

"I am thrilled to share a story of one of the greatest loves ever known, a story of bravery to dream of and then create a safe haven for like-minded individuals who wanted a place of their own. I can remember the panic that set in the first time I went to Sahara. On tour, I was new to the excitement of riding in a limo, seeing the reaction of people dancing to my music, then suddenly being told, 'This club is different.' I was unaware of what I was about to experience. 'This is a woman's club! Wink. Wink.' There was fear, anxiety, and laughter. I didn't know what to think, but in I went! Warmth, joy, happiness, and excitement greeted me at the door. My Dear Friends, still all these years later, that same warmth, joy, happiness, and excitement greets me each time we see each other. I cherish the times I spent, the lifelong friends, the celebrations, and the memories I will always hold so dear. Thank you, Leslie, for sharing your incredible story!"

—Linda Clifford, R & B and disco singer

"Leslie Cohen's writing is bold, beautiful and brutally honest. She writes as she has lived, without fear or hesitation. I find my own story woven (like so many others) through the fabric of late nights at Sahara and the blinding sunlight of 6:00 A.M. on the Upper East Side. Somehow we all survived. I am honored to be part of this history."

—Brooke Kennedy, Emmy Award–nominated television producer and director

"In *The Audacity of a Kiss*, Leslie Cohen is telling a neglected story that we all need to hear. Her club Sahara was a touchstone of feminist and LGBT history, and we're long overdue for a (re)visit."

—Michael Schiavi, professor of English at the New York Institute of Technology and author of *Celluloid Activist: The Life and Times of Vito Russo*

"Seeing Beth and Leslie's love at a young age had a profound influence on me. I remember going to their beautiful house with my mom and feeling their love in their home. It definitely shaped me at a young age as to what I could have for myself as an adult."

—Rachel Robinson, former MTV star of *Road Rules* and *The Challenge* and founder of @rachel_fitness

The Audacity of a Kiss

Frontispiece. Beth and me on the beach in East Hampton, NY, 1985, where we spent many wonderful summers. Photo credit: Adrienne Rubin.

I have lived long enough to see the rises and falls of the earth as she breathes. I have marched with women, at times hated men, and learned how to love someone more than I love myself. I have lived long enough to see the cancer of greed, the harm of lies, and the tragedy of not loving yourself. I have witnessed the death of conservatism, the joys of progressiveness, and the threat of returning to where we started. I have lived long enough to see the unthinkable, a world walking backwards.
I owe my survival to three constants: art, music, and a love so profound that it has saved two lives: hers and mine

—Kim Green

The Audacity of a Kiss

Love, Art, and Liberation

LESLIE COHEN

Rutgers University Press

New Brunswick, Camden, and Newark, New Jersey, and London

Library of Congress Cataloging-in-Publication Data

Names: Cohen, Leslie, 1947– author.
Title: The audacity of a kiss : love, art, and liberation / Leslie Cohen.
Description: New Brunswick, New Jersey : Rutgers University Press, [2021] |
    Includes bibliographical references.
Identifiers: LCCN 2020052873 | ISBN 9781978825116 (hardcover) |
    ISBN 9781978825130 (epub) | ISBN 9781978825154 (pdf)
Subjects: LCSH: Cohen, Leslie, 1947– | Segal, George, 1924–2000. Gay
    liberation. | Sahara (Nightclub : New York, N.Y.) | Lesbians—New York
    (State)—New York—Biography. | Lesbian businesswomen—New York
    (State)—New York—Biography. | Gay liberation movement—New York
    (State)—New York—History—20th century. | Public sculpture,
    American—New York (State)—New York. | Lesbian bars—New York
    (State) —New York. | New York (N.Y.)—Biography.
Classification: LCC HQ75.4.C65 A3 2021 | DDC 306.76/63092 [B]—dc23
LC record available at https://lccn.loc.gov/2020052873

A British Cataloging-in-Publication record for this book is available
from the British Library.

Copyright © 2021 by Leslie Cohen
All rights reserved.
No part of this book may be reproduced or utilized in any form or by any means,
electronic or mechanical, or by any information storage and retrieval system, without
written permission from the publisher. Please contact Rutgers University Press,
106 Somerset Street, New Brunswick, NJ 08901. The only exception to this
prohibition is "fair use" as defined by U.S. copyright law.

♾ The paper used in this publication meets the requirements of the American
National Standard for Information Sciences—Permanence of Paper for Printed
Library Materials, ANSI Z39.48-1992.

www.rutgersuniversitypress.org

Manufactured in the United States of America

For my mother, Marcia
And my wife, Beth

Love consists in this—that two solitudes protect and
touch and greet each other.
—Rainer Maria Rilke

Contents

Part III: A Posse of Outsiders

Illustrations

Author's Note

I have changed the names of some individuals in this book to protect their anonymity.

Prologue

In 1979, George Segal, the famous Pop artist, was commissioned to create a sculpture commemorating the 1969 Stonewall uprising in New York City. The uprising was the seminal, although not the only, event to kick-start the gay liberation movement. Segal's bronze sculpture, covered with a white lacquer finish, was eventually unveiled in Christopher Park in Greenwich Village, formerly known as Sheridan Square Park, in 1992, after almost thirteen years of controversy. The sculpture is called *Gay Liberation*. It depicts a life-size male couple standing a few feet away from a life-size female couple sitting together on a park bench. One of the men holds the shoulder of his friend. One of the women touches the thigh of her partner as they gaze into each other's eyes. Over the years, *Gay Liberation*, the sculpture, has become more and more recognizable around the world and an icon that is visited by thousands of people every year.

Beth Suskin, my partner (and now wife) of more than forty-five years, and I were the models for this sculpture. Since the sculpture's unveiling in 1992, we have stood before it many times, staring at our doppelganger selves. We have witnessed drunken men slouched on the park bench with their heads resting on our laps, children climbing on us like monkey bars and sitting on our knees, and grown men and women crying openly before it, overcome with emotion, because they remember the many years of humiliation they experienced when they were taunted, arrested, and forced to hide because they were gay or lesbian. Gay men and lesbians from around the world have come to see the sculpture as a symbol of gay pride and as a confirmation of the great progress that has been made towards their visibility and acceptance.

It is astounding to us that our love for one another is publicly signified and immortalized in this way. However, our love story cannot be told in full without also including the tale of Sahara, the first New York City nightclub owned by women and designed for women. I opened it with three other women in Manhattan in 1976. The club was an elegant oasis in a desert of oppression against women, both gay and straight, where women discovered a safe space to express who they were. Luminaries of the time came to witness and bask in the welcoming scene, which in turn nurtured a generation of women who would become luminaries of the future. Beth and I discovered our love for each other and nurtured it against the backdrop of Sahara, and in my mind, they are inextricably woven together. This is our story.

The Audacity of a Kiss

PART I

Youth

The only constant is confusion.
—Leslie Cohen

1

Secrets and Dreams

I was born in 1947, two years after the Hiroshima bomb and the end of World War II, the year that the Central Intelligence Agency (CIA) was formed. Jackie Robinson became the first African American to play baseball for a major league team, and the gender-bending artist, David Bowie, was born. Whatever memories I have of my earliest years are few but sweet. I played, I laughed, I skinned my knees. When I was four or five years old, I stared up at the sky one afternoon trying to see God. What appeared overhead was the enormous image of the Knickerbocker man (an image from an old beer ad of the time) in his colonial dress and three-cornered hat looming over me amongst the clouds. This appearance of what I thought was God was so real that it frightened me, and I ran into the house to find my mother.

·

In 1955, for my eighth birthday, my mother, Marcia, gave me a pink bassinet stroller. Curious, I peeked under the hood of this alien girl's toy to find a plastic doll wrapped in a blanket. I smiled and thanked my mother, not knowing what I would ever do with this oversized plaything in which I had absolutely no interest. I decided that the carriage could be useful to store my catcher's mitt, baseball, and bat when I wasn't using them. They would be safe there next to the doll that I never touched.

In the large apartment complex in Whitestone, Queens, where we lived, my play area was a paved quad, partially inhabited by a one-story parking garage and a concrete playground made up of seesaws and swings. Adjacent to the playground were rows of do-it-yourself clotheslines that sagged in the background from the weight of boxer shorts, undershirts, and bleached white bedsheets that swayed in the wind like flags of surrender. The smell of fresh detergent permeated the air around us. Corralling the quad on all sides were the indistinguishable and unadorned two-story, connected, redbrick apartment buildings. Sparse trees and grass were scattered around, but pavement underlined almost everything.

I grew up a tomboy in the 1950s. A daredevil, I spent restless summers on my bike, doing "boy things." We played stickball and "catcher's fly up" in the quad's open area. Pretending to be Roman gladiators, we fought with flying rocks and sticks. Our shields were large metal ash can covers that we absconded with from the street. As the most competitive and adventurous of my friends, I often led the charge. I was always the victor at "scissor locks," a wrestling game that allowed me to take down my opponents and lock them between my legs while lying on my back until they screamed for mercy. I won because of the impressive strength of my limbs.

Another of our favorite games was climbing man-made dirt mounds at construction sites, surrounded by the scent of dank concrete and upturned earth from newly poured foundations, a smell I loved. Fighting off the others while covered in dirt from head to foot, the rule was that whoever reached the top of the hill first was named King of the Mountain. Other times we would clamber onto the roof of the parking garage, rip off the rubber shingles, and hurl them at each other like missiles. The goal was to "mortally wound" our make-believe opponents. It was not easy to achieve, but we loved the battle.

The most fatal wound for me, however, was the onset of puberty. Before puberty, running, fighting, and proving my strength felt natural. I was equal or superior in my prowess and abilities to anyone my age, regardless of gender. With all my might I ran, biked, and flexed my budding muscles without an inkling that soon I would no longer conquer or belong.

Starting at age eleven, as my small breasts began to bud on my strong, flat frame, my bravado and self-confidence began to wane. While I was still detached from the changing contours of my unruly body, I didn't really notice that my male peers were growing stronger than me—until the day I lay wounded and sprawled on the ground, looking up at them. A fourteen-year-old boy had received a new set of boxing gloves and challenged me to a fight. What had been a typical boxing match between friends turned into the day that would forever shift my perspective.

My eleven-year-old face just wasn't prepared for the wallop it received from my opponent. The shocking pain of his punch folded me like an accordion, dropping me to the ground. Then two other boys joined in and pinned me down to further illustrate their superior strength. I struggled to rise but, with their laughter filling my ears, they held me down while their hands cupped my undeveloped breasts. Mortified, I lay there, too weak to defend myself.

Like lightning, I had been struck, not only by the force of a boy's punch but also by the cruel reality that *I was a girl* and that being a girl now presented me with physical limitations. I could not defend myself. I never faced restraints before then, at least ones that I was aware of. It would be my last competitive battle with the boys in the neighborhood and my first realization that, at least when it came to physical prowess, I was inferior. At that moment, a paradigm shifted dramatically for me, a change that would soon be accentuated by my own family dynamic and alter my life forever.

•

The 1950s and early 1960s were not the time or place to be vocal. Secrets are often the only things we can hold on to when silence is the fashion. No one ever spoke about what was right, or, for that matter, what was *wrong*. There were just expectations. I moved through my younger years with a smile on my face, totally enthralled with childhood, innocent, until adolescence blasted me.

Deciphering what I could and could not do with my changing female body disturbed me a great deal. The boundaries of possibility were already shrinking. More and more resigned, I often asked myself—did my desire to have the options and choices in life that boys had really matter? I was a girl, destined to be a housewife and a mother anyway. Perhaps that is why my mother gave me that baby stroller. It was a type of litmus test to prepare me for who I would become. I could sense that I was not expected to go out into the world and battle like the boys to make a living and have adventures. My stomach churned with a nagging discomfort at the notion of a life confined by a single limiting scenario, being a wife and mother, but any other thought was bewildering.

·

I was eleven when my father moved us from Queens to a house in Jericho, Long Island. The split-level house backed up to potato farms and was part of a subdivision called Birchwood Park Homes. I loved having a house and being close to nature. There were lots of trees to climb, so leaving Queens wasn't so bad for me. My fifteen-year-old brother, Michael, hated it.

My friends at this time, the eleven- and twelve-year-old boys and girls in Long Island, were starting to blossom into preteens, which meant they saw each other with new curiosity. To demonstrate their maturing sexuality, the boys started to engage in the pulling and plucking of girls' bra straps. In a desperate attempt to fit in, I begged my mother for a bra, which my undeveloped breasts could not fill.

However, I felt little sexual attraction to boys and couldn't relate to the suffocating hormones that flew through the air between the young girls and boys who were my friends. I was already becoming aware of the vast chasm of expectations that existed between boys and girls. My beloved bat and glove were now relegated to a shelf in my closet. Life became even more baffling as I tried to transition from perceiving boys as friends and teammates to objects of desire, and my differentness from other girls became even more pronounced, at least to me. My world had changed and I *so* wanted to fit in, to follow the prescribed path—to desire boys and have boyfriends, to be like all the other girls.

·

My mother, Marcia Cohen, and her sisters, Simi and Blanche, were the first women I loved. Of course, I loved my uncles (their

FIG. 1. Mom, cousin Charlotte, Aunt Simi, and Aunt Blanche, posing like Ziegfeld girls.

husbands), but they weren't nearly as dynamic to me as my aunts. My mother and her sisters never said it outright, but they seemed to feel the same way. The men either lacked their intelligence, joie di vivre, or integrity. My mother and aunts were all beautiful, honest, and filled with life and mischief. When we got together, they often spoke Yiddish so that I and my cousins, Bobby and

Alan (Blanche's sons), and Ellen (Simi's daughter), wouldn't understand what gossip or marriage problems they discussed.

We were all exhibitionists. Everyone wanted to perform and compete for attention. As my mother and her sisters would sing "Whatever Lola Wants, Lola Gets" or tap dance the two-step in perfect syncopation, the kids would play the kitchen pots like bongo drums and the spoons like gypsy castanets. Giggling, we made music when there was none. Being with them felt like being at a bountiful feast. With these women there was boundless love, safety, and joy.

But I also grew more conflicted as I matured, knowing that I didn't want to be like them in one major respect. The financial dependence they had on their husbands for the welfare of themselves and their children had entrapped them in unfulfilled lives and unhappy marriages, and I was determined not to let that happen to me.

I *adored* my mother; she was my best friend, my never-ending source of unconditional love, who had little choice but to do what women did in that era, which was marry young, in her case at barely eighteen years of age, and raise a family. Her father died when she was thirteen, and she no longer wanted to be a financial burden to her three older brothers, who supported her, her mother, and her sisters. My mother was 5'3" with dark hair and eyes and a swarthy Mediterranean complexion, attractive, wise, and funny. She continually watched her weight and strove to look her best because beauty was the most potent asset women of her generation utilized to advance their status in the world.

A stay-at-home mom with few marketable skills, she was petrified about not sustaining herself and her children without my father's financial support, and her fear cast a shadow over us all. She was terribly insecure, and I watched her suffer under the domination of my father, Max. I secretly despised her financial dependence on him because there were many times she should have left him and did not. Unbeknownst to her, she taught me that I did not have the luxury to dream of a prince on a white horse who would

FIG. 2. Mom and Dad in the early days.

FIG. 3. Michael and me.

whisk me away and pay my bills. That fairy tale was bogus, and the price was too high to pay. Every single day, she was living proof of the necessity of learning to provide for myself. My mother, brother, and I were desperately tethered by financial need to my father, who had left us long before he left the house.

·

In the early days of my youth, my older brother, Michael, was crazy about his little sister. But when we moved to Jericho, things changed drastically. Michael just didn't fit into suburban Long Island. He was a city kid and did not adjust well to Jericho's demanding and competitive school system.

All my father could see in Michael was disappointment, which caused him to constantly berate and smack him around. We were terrified of Max whenever he was home, threatening us with his loud voice and raised hand ready to strike. Michael turned his frustrations against me as he grew into a bitter, angry teenager. Whenever he got his hands on me, he'd torture me, beating me up for no apparent reason. I became the recipient of Michael's despair as he changed from protector to predator and reminded me of my own inability to defend myself against the physical attacks of boys and men. The tension and stress in our house were palpable.

My father wanted Michael to become a lawyer, because he thought being a professional would make his son's life easier than his own. But all the nagging and badgering backfired. Instead of becoming a lawyer, my brother, in his perpetually misguided effort to fast-track success and impress my father, became a compulsive gambler, which was to be the lifelong albatross around his neck. As I listened to him disparage my brother again and again I wondered why he did not focus any attention on me. My future was ignored even though I was the one with the potential to become what my father wanted. I wanted to scream out what about me! My father was indifferent because he just assumed I would become a wife and mother like most of the women of his generation.

Michael wanted to emulate Max. Both my parents were first generation Americans. My grandparents immigrated from the shtetls of Eastern Europe in the early part of the twentieth century. Growing up in the tenements of Manhattan's Lower East Side during the depression, Max was polishing shoes for strangers on street corners by the time he was eleven. Although Max never finished high school, as he matured over the course of the 1940s and '50s he was filled with swagger and charisma, characterized by his sharkskin suits, alligator shoes, sapphire pinky ring, and Cadillacs. He danced the mambo and sported a large anchor tattoo on his bicep from his years in the Navy during WWII. He carried a gun holster on his hip for protection.

Max owned a small jewelry store in Times Square. The store gave him prestige, but it robbed my mother of a husband and my brother and me of a father. That minuscule jewelry store where he spent most of his waking hours became the prison cell of responsibility from which he could not escape. I once overheard him say to my mother that we, his family, were the parasites who fed off him and kept him locked up there. His craving for freedom propelled him to live a separate life—with other women. "Work" was the reason he always gave to excuse his perpetual absences. Some nights he didn't come home at all.

My parents constantly fought. "What is this?" I heard my mother screaming one night through the thin walls of our split-level home. My father's muffled and angry responses were impossible to decipher. Only four-letter cusses flew out between his inaudible excuses. My mother had found a lipstick that wasn't hers in my father's car.

"Whose is it?" My mother persisted.

The smell of his cologne wafted under their bedroom door, filling the hall with his unforgettably manly scent as he quickly got dressed to leave. Sometimes the smell of his cologne was the only proof I had that he existed. Their voices rose and lowered as they fought. As he descended the stairs on his way out the door, she grabbed onto his leg and held on as he dragged her down the steps. She begged him, *"Please don't go. Max, please don't go."* The sound of her desperation tore out pieces of my heart. It pained me to see and hear how he had reduced her to a whimpering child.

•

My brother finally tipped me off, telling me the truth—that the nights I thought my father was working late, he was often dancing the mambo and the cha-cha at the famous nightclub, the Latin Quarter, around the corner from his store in Times Square. He was a great dancer. He also started an intense affair with the bandleader's wife.

One Saturday, my father took my brother and me to the jewelry store because my mother had an appointment. He said that afterward we were going to meet a "friend" for dinner at a nearby Chinese restaurant. Maria, his "friend," was a very attractive Puerto Rican woman. Sitting across the table, she frequently smiled ingratiatingly at us, trying to make a good impression, but we were smarter than that. My brother and I just looked down at our chop suey, avoiding my father's and Maria's eyes. My father's phony attentiveness to us was a clear ruse to impress his girlfriend and it made us angry and uncomfortable.

After dinner, my father drove Maria to her apartment in Queens. While she was out of the car, my father turned to us in the backseat and said, "How would you like Maria to be your mother?" We were just kids—twelve and fifteen years old. When he saw the mortified look on our faces, he turned back around. When Maria returned to the car, he drove us home to Jericho, showed her our house (in my mother's absence), his insignia of financial success, and then they drove away together. I told my mother. The look on her face made me wish I hadn't.

.

On the occasions that we visited my father's store together, my mother and I would walk hand in hand into the belly of Times Square. It was wondrous. We stood, looking up at all of the glittering neon lights and watching the rings of smoke billow out of the huge Camel cigarette billboard towering over everything. I was mesmerized by the camel's comical face and the perfectly round rings it blew out of its open mouth into the night air, which would then begin to wiggle, break up, and finally dissipate into the neon sky as a new perfectly round circle began to emerge. My mother would have to pull me away.

We would then walk to the Metropole Cafe on Seventh Avenue. Standing outside on the crowded sidewalk, we'd listen to the sounds of the then unknown Afro-Cuban jazz percussionist, Mongo Santamaría (who many consider the greatest conga drummer of the twentieth century), play on a small stage inside, the rhythmic drumbeats wafting out through the open doors to the bustling street outside. We couldn't help but move our bodies in response to the percussive beats echoing into the glittering night until we broke down laughing and returned to the store. My mother and I were best friends, but my father remained a stranger.

Only on Sundays, the one day he did not work and was home, would Max Cohen morph into his closest approximation of a "real" father. It was not a pleasant day for us. We cowered under his loud voice while he barked orders at us like a drill sergeant to pull the weeds and mow the lawn of the house that we could not afford. Threatening and abusive, he was like a domestic drone flying over our heads, looking for a target to attack, berating us for weeds that we neglected to pull.

I've always had mixed feelings about my father. I know he loved me and my brother. He did take care of us financially, but I also know he resented us for that. Until I went away to college and found out otherwise, I thought that's how fathers behaved. We take from our parents whatever they give us. It was only possible for me to take the few pieces of him that he offered. He is the reason that I have always straddled the fence between decency and rage.

•

My resentment of my brother grew over the years. When my father was convicted of trafficking in counterfeit coins and sentenced to three years in prison (of which he served one and a half years), my brother's gambling and subsequent debts became so out of hand that he started to hock anything he could find for cash. My father's jewelry that was now warehoused in a closet in our home, my mother's mink coat, and dollar bills started disappearing.

After Michael hocked one of the jewelry store watches from the closet to pay off a debt, the police showed up at our front door one day in the late afternoon and my brother and mother were taken to the police station for questioning. It turned out that the watch was "hot." I went along to support my mother because she was an extremely nervous woman who could not handle a crisis on her own and she needed me. Understandably, facing the possibility that her husband and son were involved in a criminal act was too much for her to bear alone. Even though I was only thirteen years old, I was more capable of remaining composed and levelheaded than she was. It was an inner strength that I have always had. I'm not sure if it was something I inherently developed to cope with these upheavals in my family life or whether I was born with it. Nature or nurture? Who knows?

After spending hours at the police station explaining that they had no idea that the watch from my father's store was stolen, my mother and brother were allowed to go home. That was one of the toughest nights of my life because my mother totally imploded when we arrived back at the house. She was afraid that my father would have to serve more time in jail for dealing in stolen property. She was inconsolable, thrashing in her bed, hysterical, and there was nothing I could do to calm her down. I called my Aunt Blanche, who drove out to Jericho from Queens. She gave my mother a tranquilizer, talked her down, and was finally able to put her to sleep. Fortunately, the police did not pursue the matter, and nothing ever came of it, but it was clear to my parents that something had to be done with Michael. To put an end to the gambling and the problems that it caused, my parents decided to enlist him in the Air Force. Ironically, my brother would not finish high school, the one thing that my father wanted the most for him. Eventually, however, he did receive his GED diploma.

With an absentee father and my brother now out of the house, my mother and I were a mutual preservation society, loving each other unconditionally and desperately trying to preserve what was left of the family. Many years later, my brother told me that my mother was able to financially survive my father's absence during his imprisonment with the help of the Mob, with whom he had apparently worked, and who left us a paper bag filled with cash at our front door.

During this time, I was living a dual life: a popular girl at school, all smiles, with lots of friends, but totally secretive about my home life. No one knew of my travails. My suburban girlfriends were my unwitting saviors from total despair, distracting me with our childhood crushes, playing seven minutes in heaven with the boys, making out, and dancing to our collection of 78 and 45 rpm records. The continual closeness of my aunts and cousins helped too. But watching my mother's pain during those years ignited righteousness in me that I still wear on my sleeve.

•

Eventually, after his release from prison, my father started a new business: installing underground sprinkler systems for suburban homeowners, which ultimately became quite successful. We sold the house to relieve him of some of the financial strain during that time and moved from Jericho back into an apartment in Fresh Meadows, Queens (absent my brother, who was now in the Air Force).

By the time I entered Francis Lewis High School in 1962, there was a tentative optimism in the air, both in my household, because my father was home and attentive to my mother, and in the world, as John F. Kennedy became our thirty-fifth president. Kennedy was the youngest man to hold that office, and his election brought a fresh perspective to the country and the world.

On the other hand, the racial divide was ripping the country apart. That year, the integrated group of civil rights activists called the Freedom Riders boldly drove buses through the South, protesting segregated bus terminals. Their peaceful act of protest created a new tidal wave of racial hatred. The images of bloody bodies strewn through the streets covered the evening news. The injustice deeply affected and angered me. I embraced folk music protest artists like Phil Ochs, Peter, Paul and Mary, Buffy Sainte-Marie, and Joan Baez. I learned the guitar and earnestly sang their songs. The momentum of change was hitting the world from both sides, creating hope, confusion, and a deep fear of things unseen. Although there were spurts of change everywhere, the only groundbreaking change for women was the unveiling of Pampers, the first disposable diapers. Women still had a long way to go.

•

My father's new business was doing well, and he hired a young British secretary, only three years older than my brother, to assist him. After a while, they began to have an affair and he eventually moved in with her. So, once again, it was just my mother and me. The two of us existed in survival mode, constantly worrying about money and wondering what the next catastrophe would be. Once again, I had to be the strong one, but I was no longer climbing dirt mounds. I was caring for the remains of a family that had fallen apart.

FIG. 4. Me and Michael on a visit with my father after he and my mother had separated and he was living with his girlfriend.

My mother, trying to find herself among the ruins of her marriage of twenty-three years, finally started a new life. Now that I was in high school and she was separated from my father, she began to date men for the first time. God knows, she deserved it. However, my heart was so inextricably linked to hers that, instead of encouraging her efforts, the idea of her trying to find love from someone other than me was devastating. I did not want a stranger entering our lives. My brother was stationed in Biloxi, Mississippi; my father lived with his girlfriend; and my mother, my anchor, was dating and spending less and less time with me. I thought I was in her way, that I was no longer her best friend but instead a burden to her. It felt like everyone had abandoned me. I was sixteen years old and can safely say I have never, before or since, felt such profound loneliness.

I nearly came undone and was very close to an emotional breakdown. I was extremely fragile at the time, but also determined to survive. I don't know where that inner strength came from, but I found the will to keep going. No one, especially my own family, would destroy me. "No one's going to get me," I repeated to myself over and over. From the outside, I looked as if I was holding everything together, still popular and outgoing at school, but in reality, my insides were eating themselves and I was fighting a ferocious battle. It was a very different time then. Families did not split apart. Divorce was anathema. I was too ashamed to tell my friends what was going on. I didn't want to be ostracized or pitied. No one could detect that every day, after school, I returned to my own private hell.

The very idea that my mother would date other men and leave me alone drove me insane. The one time I heard her kissing a date good night at our apartment door, we viciously fought and I cruelly called her a whore. It was heartbreaking for both of us because we loved each other so deeply. We both needed to separate and find our own way.

It was during this unsettling period when my parents separated and then divorced that the inequities that existed in our society because of gender roles became painfully tangible to me. I watched as some of my mother's friends, who were separated or divorced from their husbands, suffered even more than my mother did because of the financial straits they were left in when their husbands left. The pitfalls of the "Mad Men" era required men to be breadwinners who were not capable of doing so. Burdened beyond their abilities, these men fled and abandoned their wives and children, leaving them nearly destitute. The women, who were trained only to be mothers and housewives, their roles fortified by the laws that forbade them gaining financial independence for themselves, had to take menial jobs that paid little, yet they still had to support themselves and their children. It was terribly unfair and left a visceral impression on me that would sometimes, years later, turn into indignation. That's why, no matter what my father had done, and as limited as our funds were, I was always grateful to him for financially supporting and not abandoning me.

·

As afraid as I was to ask for financial help, I did tell my father I aspired to go to an out-of-town college. It was something I was determined to do. It was my way out, my road to sanity. My father agreed to pay for me to attend a low-cost state teachers' college but added that he would then cut my mother off financially since I was the only reason he was still supporting us at all. I refused to be part of anything that would further impoverish my mother. She had found a job as a file clerk in the city and was making the grueling trip every day by bus but we were still living hand to mouth. My love and devotion for my mother could not be challenged. To see her struggling to make a living without any practical experience was hard enough. I would never abandon her.

The news that my father had impregnated his mistress was the final straw for my mother, while at the same time giving us a way out of our financial dilemma. After some relentless prodding from me to convince her that divorcing my father was the only way she would be financially protected, she finally found the courage to hire an attorney. My father's egregious transgression as a still-married man legally guaranteed us some income. With child support, college loans, help from my father, and various jobs, I managed to go away to college.

2

Confetti on New Year's Eve

In the staggering heat of August 1965, my mother and my best friend, Lois, accompanied me on the 400-mile drive from Bayside, Queens, to Buffalo State College, where I was to begin my freshman-year orientation. It was a teachers' college and, like most young women of that era, given the limited choices available, I planned to become a high school history teacher. My mother was relieved when Lois agreed to come along so that she wouldn't have to be alone for the long ride home.

As we slowly progressed along our eight-hour trek to Buffalo, my mind wandered as I imagined what the future would hold for me. In college, I was actually going to be my own person, no longer defined by my absent father, my gambling brother, and my frightened, anxiety-ridden mother. As we drove, the trees became more bountiful and I couldn't stop humming the Four Tops song "I Can't Help Myself (Sugar Pie, Honey Bunch)." Remembering a time with my father, I hummed the chorus over and over again.

My father's high school graduation gift to me had been taking me out on a real father-daughter date. He had picked me up in his white Cadillac convertible with its red leather interior, handed me the keys to drive, and took me to the Copacabana nightclub to see the Four Tops, live. I knew he was very proud of me for graduating high school.

My father hardly knew me as a young adult because we saw each other so infrequently during my high school years. The last time

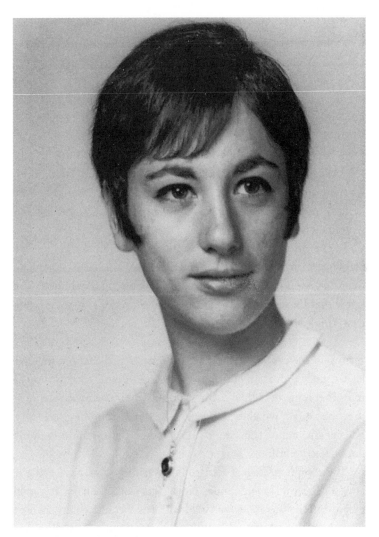

FIG. 5. My high school graduation, 1965.

he saw me all dressed up was years before I became a teenager. I wanted to impress my father and show him how grown-up I had become. Wearing a dress and high heels, I got all made-up in pink lipstick and black eyeliner. When we stepped into the Copacabana, he waved to some friends he knew who had initially thought I was his date, until he proudly introduced me to them as his daughter.

Like me, Max's mood improved whenever there was music. As we found our seats in the club, *the* Smokey Robinson and *the* Berry Gordy of Motown sat down at the table next to us. They were heroes to me, and I excitedly told my father who they were. After a couple of songs, my father asked me to dance. In high school, I had been known as "the dancer" (I had won "Best Dancer" in the senior personality contest in our graduating class of over 1,500 seniors), so I was happy to oblige. When the Four Tops launched into their hit song "I Can't Help Myself (Sugar Pie, Honey Bunch)" that night, I belted out the chorus. My father looked at me lovingly as we danced, proud of his daughter who was going off to college and who knew the words to the song.

In the car with my mother and Lois, I smiled at the memory of being with him. It was the only time we had ever been alone together. Inaudibly, I whispered, "Sugar pie, honey bunch/You know that I love you," and hummed the addictive chorus. Despite everything he put us through, I loved him.

•

Sitting in the center of the quiet, upstate city, Buffalo State College stretched over an enormous 125 acres of land. The canopy of trees that hung over the bustling campus contrasted with the sun-drenched quad, which was enclosed by the surrounding residence halls at the end of the campus. We parked the car and found my dorm, Perry Hall.

The reception area of Perry Hall was devoid of any aesthetic appeal. The walls were cinder block and painted an institutional green, and the furniture was drab, with couches and chairs covered in orange Naugahyde. The only thing that made it inviting was the smiling faces of the older girls who were there to greet us. An attractive, slender, dark-haired woman named Barbara, a sophomore, sat behind the welcome desk. When we walked towards her, she must have seen the angst on my mother's face. She looked over my papers and told me my room was only a few doors down from hers. She grabbed my hand from across the desk and winked at my mother. "Don't worry, I'll take care of her," she said. My mother's

FIG. 6. Mom and me the first day we arrived at Buffalo State College, 1965; the deep love between us is apparent.

tight worried face started to relax. She smiled gratefully at Barbara and looked away.

I was assigned a roommate whose name, Sharon, was on the same piece of paper as my room number. When Lois, my mother, and I first peeked inside the door of my room, Sharon wasn't there yet. The room held two single beds, two dressers, and two desks with chairs. It was plain and colorless but I couldn't care less. We closed the door and unpacked my things. My mother carefully

FIG. 7. Lois and me horsing around on the first day we arrived at Buffalo State College, 1965.

folded and placed my clothes into the dresser across from my bed. Lois joked about future frat parties and the many boyfriends that I would have. My mother and I, both of us lost in our heads, dreamt of what would come next for each of us in this new chapter of our lives.

After all of my belongings were put away, my mother suggested that we spend the rest of the afternoon exploring the campus. As we walked the hallway, each room that we passed held a scene similar to the one we just left: nervous parents and freshmen unpacking trunks and suitcases.

I smiled awkwardly at girls and parents of all shapes and sizes as they passed us in the hall. When we reached the end of the building, we exited Perry Hall and walked into the sun. Just ahead of us was a door to another nondescript three-story brick building, exactly the same, facing the quad. We entered, walking past more open dorm rooms. Suddenly, my mother stopped short at an open doorway and eyed me with a knowing look. I felt a shift in her demeanor. *Uh-oh.*

She had picked up familiar accents drifting out of the room: New York Jews, kindred spirits, descendants of the shtetls. Their voices triggered in her the profound connection between Jewish people that excited her to no end. Before I could stop her, she stuck her head into the open doorway. The girl's parents looked up from the large trunk they were unpacking as they wondered who this stranger peering into their daughter's room could be. Their reserve had absolutely no effect on my mother, who proceeded to greet them as if they were long-lost cousins. It seemed then that the other parents' tribal instincts slowly kicked in, too. In an instant they were trading vital statistics.

"Where are you from?" the other mother asked my mom.

My mother responded, "New York—Queens. And you?"

"Hewlett Harbor."

"*Reeeeally?*" My mother could not hide her delight at meeting people who lived in the familiar, well-to-do community on the South Shore of Long Island.

"Did you just arrive?" my mother asked.

"Yes," the girl's mother said, distracted by their daughter, who had been giving her parents instructions about where to put her belongings.

Too preoccupied with unpacking the large trunk in front of her, the daughter still had her head buried and didn't seem to care that we were in the room. Her mother called her daughter's name softly in order to make her aware that she had visitors, but she remained distracted. Her name was Beth. My mother comfortably started to use it as if she knew the girl.

"So, is Beth a freshman, too?"

"Yes," her mother said.

"Oh, maybe you girls can be friends," my mother said. My mother pulled me closer. Looking directly at Beth, she said, "Beth, this is my daughter, Leslie . . . wouldn't it be nice if the two of you became friends?"

As she lifted her face to me, I was taken aback. She was strikingly beautiful—high cheekbones, a strongly defined jawline, full lips, perfectly straight teeth, and olive-green eyes that slanted slightly upward. Her thick straight eyebrows perfectly complemented her face. She was dressed in a straight skirt to her knees, simple pumps, a cashmere sweater, and pearls. She had this European elegance to her, comparable to European movie stars like Catherine Deneuve and Ursula Andress that I so admired at the time. Our eyes met for the first time as we both nodded uncomfortably. I felt myself blush as we exchanged self-conscious smiles. After exchanging some pleasantries, I was eager to move on.

"I'm sure I'll see you on campus," I said as I gently shoved my mother out of the door. Beth was the first freshman I met.

At last, it was time for my mother and Lois to get back on the road for the long trip back to Queens. At the car, I gave my mother a long embrace, promising that I would be okay and that I'd call often. A sharp sadness came over us both as we, who were so fundamentally attached to each other for so many years, said our goodbyes. And Lois—I was wishing that she could stay so we could continue to experience the world together. We hugged and I promised to call often.

•

As the days passed, I familiarized myself with the campus and college life. Though my roommate, Sharon, who grew up in a small upstate New York town, was pleasant enough, we never became close. That was okay because, as it turned out, she found her own friends and I found mine, the New York City and Long Island girls with a conscientious fashion flair and a very specific gregariousness and accent.

Barbara, who greeted us that first day of freshman orientation, and I actually did become close friends. Playfully physical, she was always pulling me onto her lap and kissing my neck. I realized that while I totally relished her affection and returned it wholeheartedly,

FIG. 8. Beth in high school in 1965 in Hewlett, Long Island, posing for her art teacher. This is what she looked like when we met at Buffalo State College.

I was slightly uncomfortable because, as it turned out, her play-fulness sometimes turned me on. Without having a name for what we were doing, I loved the intimacy but had a hard time admitting it to myself.

Being with Barbara unwittingly reminded me of other close encounters with girls that I had at camp and in high school. My mind would not allow me to linger on the memory of the high school friend who had visited me at the apartment where I lived with my mother, and, while we lay together talking on my bed, rubbed her crotch against my leg. At the time, I quickly pulled away and ignored it as if it had never happened. The same was true of the memory of Susan from camp. We became inseparable. I must have been in love with her. Why else would my knees have buckled when she held my body close to hers in her bunk or when we hid in the bathroom stall to embrace? Why did my heart break when she said we couldn't do that anymore because, even though she loved me, it "repulsed her"? After that, I questioned why I would still long for her and surreptitiously stare at her photograph under my desk in my eleventh grade trigonometry class.

Why did Susan find our love so wrong? The reality was, it made perfect sense for her to be ashamed of our feelings because, when we were coming of age in the 1950s and early '60s, lesbianism was completely taboo. Lesbians were considered deviant psychopaths who ended up alone, miserable, scorned by society, and suicidal. Our love had to remain buried or we would have been totally ostracized by society. No wonder she backed away. I couldn't deal with it at all and so I didn't, but still, the thoughts and feelings lingered there in the recesses of my mind like an unending fog.

•

Although I made many new friends in college, like Barbara, I spent a lot of time freshman year with Beth Suskin, the young woman I met that first day of orientation with my mom and Lois. She was so intriguing. She was definitely different than anyone else I knew. She walked like a ballet dancer, standing erect with a slight sway, and I thought she was sultry and mysterious but totally without pretense. With her cashmere sweaters, straight skirts, and pearls, she had this incredible, effortless allure. Everyone was attracted to her and wanted to know her.

Once we began spending time together, it was clear that we had more in common than I thought. We were both running away from homes that we wanted to escape, although for different reasons. When I went away to college, I felt like a battle-fatigued soldier who had served back-to-back tours and needed a long leave. My mother and father had been at war for years and my life consisted of dealing with one familial upheaval after another.

Beth left home to rid herself of her deep obsession with her mentally and emotionally abusive boyfriend, Sean, with whom she fell madly in love at the age of twelve. Like so many first loves, it was an all-encompassing passion that scrambled her senses, judgment, and reasoning. Her obsession also worked as a shield against a world she found frightening. By burying herself in her love for Sean, she found a place to hide from the onslaught of life. She came to Buffalo State to try to free herself.

I told Beth about my parents' recent divorce, and how close I was to my mother. I also told her about my strained relationship with my brother, Michael, and how much I had feared my absentee father. Beth's life was the same but different. Her father was a kind, gentle man who was also not around much while she was in high school. At the age of forty-one, he had gone back to school, completing a dental degree at the Harvard School of Dental Medicine. Both of us were raised by our mothers during our high school years.

Beth called herself a wild child, which is how I saw myself. What did that mean? To us, it meant that we did not want to be told what to do. We were reacting against the hypocrisies of the 1950s and early 1960s. We were starting to fight against the imperatives of a society that did not make sense to us. Beth described her mother as traditional and conservative; she wanted Beth to be a reflection of her—elegant, manicured, impeccably dressed, proper, and a devoted follower of the societal rule book. She wanted to control Beth, but that was not who Beth was or what she wanted, and they were clearly at odds.

"I'm attracted to new and different things," she said. "I don't want to be controlled by *her*," she would shout in frustration. Her declarations bounced off the walls around us. "I want my life to make sense to me. I don't care if it makes sense to my mother, or anyone else."

When Beth spoke like that, I knew we had a deep connection, a shared rebelliousness and a desire to be our true selves, whatever that might turn out to be. I loved the sound of her voice, which hypnotized me as it ebbed and flowed like a wave. She was a cauldron of fire and intensity. However, everything she said led back to Sean, the troubled young man she had been madly in love with since she was twelve years old. She was still obsessed with him.

Although it seemed that we were both running away from home, it was actually Beth's mother who, because she couldn't stand Sean, suggested Beth go away to college to see if she could handle a life away from him. And for some reason, that time she listened to her mother. Yet it did not seem to change her feelings for Sean. So much of our time together was spent with Beth chronicling her all-encompassing passion for this guy. Her desire for him caged her in.

I had never heard anyone talk about another person with such raw craving and heartache. She was so conflicted between her love and sexual attraction for him and her desire to break free from his possessive control. All I knew was that I was strongly drawn to her. And she was equally drawn to me and *only* me. She had no interest in being friends with anyone else. It was a curious friendship. I wondered why such a stunning woman, who could be with anyone she wanted, spent so much time alone with me, sharing her most personal secrets. Yet, I was flattered.

I tried to understand Beth's love for Sean. As we talked, I posed straightforward questions.

"Do you think that Sean tries to control you?"

"Yes!" she exclaimed, and then elaborated: "He is controlling and insanely jealous."

"Why do you stay with him, then?" I asked, pushing a little harder.

Slightly embarrassed, she said, "I just *can't* free myself of him. I keep thinking, if he only knows how much I love him, he will change. He would trust me. But it doesn't seem to make a difference."

I wanted to feel that strongly for a man. I wanted to be in love. But I just did not seem to connect with men in that way. I went on dates, but it didn't feel natural. I was so ill at ease. The guys I went out with were boys—they seemed so immature, silly, and insincere, like all they wanted was to sexually "score." Maybe I just needed to meet an older guy? I couldn't figure it out. My questions remained unanswered and I continued to hope that one day passion and love would engulf me like it had for so many of my friends.

Over the next few months, Beth and I became very close. Beth desperately needed someone to talk to about Sean and I needed to be in the presence of this new friend, a need that I had yet to understand. Beth spoke of her intense sexual desire for Sean, which I could not begin to fathom. I listened to what she said, trying to make sense of it for myself.

Her life was not easy because of her social awkwardness, and this possibly explained why she only wanted to spend time with me. She recalled, "I remember being in elementary school and wanting to participate but always having a hard time. One-on-one communication was much easier than being in a group. I didn't like to talk in class nor have people look at me. Maybe, to compensate for my social discomfort, I was boy crazy."

Her subsequent stories of kissing boys in the second and third grade and going steady with Charlie Weinstein in the sixth grade, wearing his ID bracelet, dancing close to him, and smelling his hair tonic as she buried her nose in his hair, left my mind blank. The more I heard, the more I was forced to question my own missing sexual history.

She said, "I met Sean in the summer between eighth and ninth grades and fell madly in love. I was ready to have children when I was thirteen years old. I wanted five children by the time I was fifteen and wanted to live on a farm with animals walking into my house while I cooked for my husband and children, my husband loving me, and me singing songs and dancing, always singing songs and dancing. That is who I was as a young girl."

She referred to herself as the Jewish Loretta Lynn! Her fairy tale fantasy was totally divorced from reality. When she said things like that, I just chalked it up to her naïveté, her fantastical imagination, and her wild child persona. But the more I listened, the more I learned that she meant these statements with all of her heart. I couldn't grasp what she was saying because, when I was thirteen years old, I wanted totally different things. I wanted to be competitive—playing sports, outrunning boys, zooming past them on my bike, jamming on the brakes, swirling in circles in the sand at the end of the block. Boys, for me, were equals, teammates, and my greatest adversaries. When sexual desire entered the picture, I lost my way. I listened to Beth with a touch of awe, all the while feeling the itch of my "differentness," which I still couldn't identify.

•

Ours was an unusual friendship—it was loving, deeply sensual, and fun, but it was also mysterious and confusing. We did not socialize with other friends. We spent all our time alone with each other. When we were together in our insulated world, it was both strange and wonderful. It was like the air currents around us slowed down, became electrified. Everything we did together had this otherworldly charge to it, like we were in some sort of radioactive bubble.

The magnetic force that held us together was our unspoken and unrealized attraction for each other that created that elusive, charged atmosphere. Back in 1965, we did not understand this. Not only was I sexually naive and totally inexperienced but being gay was not something I knew was possible. Same-sex love was not discussed or acknowledged by *anyone* at that time unless it was in a derogatory fashion.

Beth had been sexually active for most of her teenage life. I hadn't even gotten close. The thought that I might be a lesbian was not exactly a thought I wanted to linger on. Rather, I jumped away from those thoughts as quickly as if my hand had accidentally touched a flame on the stove. This freed Beth and me to stay in our own hidden world, where no visitors were allowed. Once again, as with my previous girl passions, I couldn't accept or act on the intensity that we felt for each other, but it was tangible.

·

Beth told me that she sang professionally in high school. She was the lead singer for a well-known local band called the Valiants. They played all the Long Island beach clubs and I had actually heard of them. I shared that I had been voted "Best Dancer" by my high school class. Since my sexual life was virtually nonexistent, I expressed my sexual energy through dancing. I reveled in the attention I received. Music and dancing became the way Beth and I were intimate without being cognizant of what we were doing. We were hiding not only from others but also from ourselves.

We both loved rhythm and blues—the old Motown and Stax sounds—and jazz. Singing and dancing to Otis Redding's mid-tempo song "(Sittin' on) the Dock of the Bay" was a favorite activity, especially when we came to the whistling part. Neither of us could whistle like Otis, but we tried so hard, until we cried from laughter. Sam and Dave's "Soul Man" was another song we loved, dancing and singing aloud with their rambunctious declaration, "*I'm a soul man!*"

We loved the music written or sung by African American artists, and that became the one way I could connect to the Black students on campus. I had been involved with the civil rights movement since high school and I marched in Harlem to protest the atrocities that happened in Selma, Alabama. Dancing offered me a partial entrée to their world. My friend Otis called me Snow as we cavorted together on the dance floor. He joked, "What color are your pigments, girl?" I was the white girl who was allowed into their party, for a while at least. But when the Black Power movement emerged out of the civil rights struggle, the Black and the white students on campus no longer hung out together, even on the dance floor. I understood the separatist movement, the yell of "I'm Black and I'm proud," but as a white ally I was shut out.

Together, Beth and I listened to R & B music and danced constantly in my dorm room. To help students avoid the frigid

Buffalo weather, the campus was fully equipped with underground tunnels that connected the dormitories so we didn't have to venture outside. The tunnels had incredible acoustics and we often went there to jam. The passageways became our own private sound studio.

One night, I played my bongo drums while Beth sang "Summertime" from the opera *Porgy and Bess*. It was a song she had sung with her band in high school. Her bluesy, sultry voice was so melodious that it filled the air, reverberating and bouncing off the tunnel's cinder block walls. Whenever she sang that song, I would close my eyes and listen to the soulful emotions that came out of her mouth. She would elongate every syllable, giving each one its own nuance. The haunting song was jazzy and terribly sad at the same time. I was so impressed by her talent and so moved that she was able to unfold in front of me.

Then we would change tempo. Beth guffawed watching me do my James Brown dance imitation, where I shuffled across the tunnel floor with one leg raised off the ground. At the top of our lungs, we would both wail "Papa's got a brand new bag," the song's title, then mimic the sound of the addictive horn section. Brown's raspy voice and the jerky cadence of the horns made our pelvises move in and out to the rhythm. The exhilaration caused me to suggest that we spray-paint "James Brown Lives!" in large red letters across the length of the tunnel wall, so that night, we did.

We fled the scene of the crime when we thought we heard someone coming. We grabbed the spray paint and bongos and ran wild-eyed out of the tunnel, laughing. It was the typical way that I lived my life. Any authoritative body that tried to curb my freedom got the salute, my metaphorical middle finger raised in the air. After years of cowering under my father's iron rule, it was my mission to take command of my own life, and that is how I did it—with my impetuous impulses and my middle finger.

Next, I decided Beth and I were going to sneak out of the dorms after curfew and go to a nightclub to dance in downtown Buffalo. My risky behavior frightened Beth but she agreed to sneak out with me. One night, after the 11:00 P.M. curfew when the dorms were locked down, I went to her room through the underground tunnels. Together we climbed out of a basement window, made it to the bus stop, and hopped on a bus headed downtown to the club. The streets of Buffalo were dark and empty. Beth's eyes were wide with fear and mine were lit with mischief and daring.

We entered the dark club after avoiding the eyes of the bouncer who let us in. We scampered down a flight of narrow stairs into a purple-lit room with a raised dance floor. It was the middle of the week, and there was hardly anyone there. Beth and I found our way to the bar where we ordered Seven and Sevens. The purple lights ricocheted off Beth's face, accentuating her cheekbones and mouth. Then we got up to dance, where we lost ourselves in the rhythms of the music and being together. "When I'm with you, I feel calm and safe," Beth said. I smiled. I knew she did, even though it was a mystery to both of us as to why. In my presence, she showed her true self, one no one else had the privilege of knowing. That night, there was no other place that I'd rather have been, or person I'd rather have been with.

Another time, lying next to me in my single bed, Beth spooned me from behind, playing with the back of my hair. She whispered, "Your hair is so beautiful. It reminds me of Sean's." There was something in the intimacy of that remark that made me feel awkward and uneasy—a bit frightened—because Beth was so naturally sexual, and she was pressed up against me. I was afraid of what she might try to do to me. I was grateful nothing happened because I was not ready, but I never forgot it.

•

Over time, as much as I loved being with Beth, I became frustrated by the fact that she refused to hang out with my other friends. When I was with Beth, I was cut off and isolated. Beth wore her pain and longing for Sean like a protective second skin insulating her from the outside world. Resentments about her need to be alone with me and the effect of this responsibility on me as her only friend started to percolate.

My other friends were very social. They were fun loving and open to new experiences, to being out in the world. Being with them in a group reminded me of the many happy times during my childhood that I spent together with my mother, my aunts, and my cousins. The other girls and I partied together, more often than I sensed Beth wanted me to, meeting guys at beer blasts and fraternity parties. The New York City and Long Island contingent was a little boy crazy and, of course, Beth had no place there, not with her preoccupation with Sean. As much as I tried, there was nothing I could do to change that.

The freedom of that first year at college with my new friends, away from my parents' travails, was joyous. I felt like confetti on New Year's Eve. I was totally carefree and elated. I danced all the time—at every bar, college dance, and fraternity beer blast I could find. I was full of mischief and life. I was on my own.

As much as I cared for Beth, her strangling need to be alone with me, coupled with her persistent gloominess and longing for Sean, slowly drove me away. I was finished with the darkness of my youth. I did not want to go back there. By the end of my freshman year, I made a conscious decision. To keep her melancholy and depression at bay, I would have to let Beth go.

3

Touching God

When we returned to school for our sophomore year, Beth and I had become strangers. I had consciously pulled away from her over the summer, but we never discussed it. There was just a chasm. The separation was difficult because I missed her and, even worse, she missed me and didn't have other friends to fall back on. I hated hurting her. Passing her in the halls, in the brief moment that our eyes met, I could see her confusion, her questioning look, as if she were asking, *What happened to us? What did I do?* Our tentativeness and immaturity left us too unprepared to understand what had transpired between us, so we didn't speak. Silence was all we had left.

•

Adrienne Rubin from Laurelton, Queens, became my roommate sophomore year. Her father was a waiter and, like me, she was always financially strapped. We became the best of friends. In 1966, my pals and I were still going to wild, drunken fraternity parties and beer blasts, a continuation of the college culture of the 1950s and early 1960s.

One night after a frat party, we all gathered back in our communal dorm bathroom to console Adrienne, who was crying and wiping away her tears as she scrubbed her deeply stained blue foot in the bathroom sink. As it turned out, while she was dancing in the middle of the crowded, beer-soaked floor of the frat house social room that night, she suddenly felt her foot becoming soaked, as if she had stepped in a puddle. When she looked down and noticed a stream hitting her shoe, she naturally followed the perfect arc from her shoe to its source, which was one very inebriated guy with his dick out pissing high into the air, the urine shooting like a guided missile directly into the opening of her brand-new blue suede shoes. Her shoes were now ruined and her foot colored a deep blue. We tried hard to console her as she scrubbed her foot in the sink, but each time we looked at her cerulean foot, the comical absurdity of what had happened grabbed us and we were unable to contain our belly laughing.

•

To furnish our bland dorm room, I stole lamps from the university lobby and painted them to disguise them. The thrill of doing something wrong was getting away with it. Finally, though, the shenanigans stopped when I was caught. After they found the lamps, I was called to the residential assistant's room, where she reprimanded me with a long-winded lecture that I didn't pay attention to, except for the last and most important part: "Leslie, you'd better get your head on straight or you'll have to go home." That sobered me right up.

I didn't want to go back to Queens and the family turmoil that I had escaped. I wanted to accomplish something in my life, and obtaining a college education was a necessity in my mind to furthering that goal. If I got kicked out of school, my dream for my future would probably end and that was a horrifying thought to me. From then on, the stealing and vandalizing stopped. I looked for exploits that wouldn't get me expelled.

There was an international study program at Buffalo State College intended for juniors called the Experiment in International Living. I applied early, as a sophomore, because I wanted to get away from campus and have a meaningful adventure that would impact me in a visceral way. If chosen, I would live with an Italian family and study Italian art, culture, and history at the University of Siena. One of the requirements for the program was that applicants had to learn Italian, which I did, and I was accepted.

In Italy, I would have the opportunity to immerse myself in art and architecture. Buried beneath the complexities of my young life, art had become my secret companion. Being around art gave me an elegant place to escape to when my life was too challenging. In high school, I regularly took the subway to the Museum of Modern Art. As an emotionally struggling young person, that's where my heart led me. I planted myself in front of Monet's *Water Lilies*, my eyes glazed over, drinking up every inch of the scene. The paintings were very large and immersive and, as I sat on the bench in the middle of the room observing them, they surrounded me. There, I could submerge myself in the blue waters and lily pads that Monet saw in his gardens at Giverny. There were no horizon lines in these paintings, so one could be totally enveloped in them. Totally lost in the colors, I could actually feel the cool water swallowing me up until I couldn't breathe and had to flee the room.

When the opportunity to study in Italy arose, there was no question that I wanted to study abroad more than anything else in the world. I wanted it so badly that I once again found the fortitude to ask my father for the 500 dollars I needed to pay for both the trip and tuition. I was petrified, but he said yes. It turned out to be the most phenomenal experience of my young life.

•

At the University of Siena, I studied Italian art, history, and culture and spent much of my time visiting cathedrals and museums. When walking into these stunning edifices, I felt transformed. Looking at all of the magnificent creations reinforced my belief that art was a reflection of the best that mankind had to offer. The boundaries of my mind and heart dissolved in the midst of the splendor. If there was a God, which I had doubted because of all the pain that existed in the world, this was his presentation, transmitted to us through human beings' artistic creations.

I visited the Museo Civico in Siena and the Brancacci Chapel in Florence with its spectacular frescoes by the early Renaissance master, Masaccio, but my favorite site was the medieval masterpiece, the Siena Cathedral, with its magnificent Romanesque and Gothic style architecture and black and white stripes etched into the marble inside and outside of the building, detailed and intricate. The endlessly soaring ceilings and meticulously designed inlaid marble mosaic floors were unforgettable, the most magnificent floors ever made. The sheer glory of that church lifted me and everything else around it. I stood back in awe and thought, *look at what human beings can do. Look at the ecstasy reflected in their talent and art.* Until then, I hadn't believed in religion. Art became my religion, my first true encounter with the spirit of God.

•

When I returned to campus for my junior year in the fall of 1967, after my travels in Europe, Beth was gone. She had transferred to Hofstra University, a college on Long Island, so she could be near Sean. It wasn't a surprise. Beth was clearly possessed by him and I had abandoned her. But for years after, I never stopped thinking and wondering about her.

•

Although I had extended my interest in art from Italian Renaissance, Baroque, and medieval art to contemporary art through the extraordinary contemporary collection at the Albright-Knox Art Gallery across the street from the campus, my love affair with art expanded into completely new mediums due to my encounter with the Merce Cunningham Dance Company, which took up residency on campus in early 1968. I only had a limited knowledge of modern dance and classical ballet, but there was something about the experimentation and "newness" of Merce Cunningham's modern dance that, like my recent discovery of modernism and abstract painting, touched a deep chord in me—a shared sense of adventure that made me want to explore these burgeoning interests further.

I was mesmerized by my first glimpse of the dancers as they practiced. Their synchronized awkward movements, so different from classical ballet, broke boundaries. The lines that their arms and legs drew were as perfectly executed as the brushstrokes of a master painter. I was captured by the innovation of their movement in Cunningham's choreography. I couldn't get enough of them, so I watched the company rehearse whenever I could.

Studying in general wasn't that essential to me. However, good grades were important to me because of the doors they would open in the future. I was a champion last-minute crammer, and my courses thus far had consisted of memorizing information and then spitting back the material. That was my formula for receiving good grades, which I did. I found that I was much more interested in learning about art and creative people. The way they broke boundaries appealed to me.

After my time in Italy, I dove headfirst into learning everything I could about art. I decided to change my major from secondary education to liberal arts so I could study art history. My discovery of modernism through the abstract paintings at the Albright-Knox Art Gallery gave me even more exposure to the contemporary art scene. I was taken by artists like Arshile Gorky, Clyfford Still, Helen Frankenthaler, and Jasper Johns, among others. They were breaking all the rules of the art world.

Not only was I enthralled with Cunningham's choreography, I was also attracted to the unusual music that he danced to. It turns out that Merce Cunningham's romantic partner, John Cage, created the unique sounds that accompanied his dances. Along with his artistic director, Jasper Johns, and artists Marcel Duchamp and Andy Warhol, they shone a whole new light on mixed media art and became the forefathers of the avant-garde art scene that put the city of Buffalo, New York, on the map in the late 1960s. I wanted to be a part of it all.

Desiring to soak up every ounce of this creativity but lacking the funds to buy tickets to the shows, I volunteered to work as an usher for as many performances as I could. The works that premiered while I was in school were *RainForest* and *Walkaround Time*. Both pieces reflected Cunningham's love for experimental staging, costuming, sets, and choreography.

RainForest had a pioneering electronic score by composer David Tudor. The set was minimalist and absolutely groundbreaking, consisting of Andy Warhol's shiny silver Mylar cloud pillows that floated randomly above the dancers' heads at each performance such that no two performances were the same. *Walkaround Time*, a tribute to artist Marcel Duchamp, was a slow-motion dance with a set created by Jasper Johns and based on Marcel Duchamp's art installation known as *The Large Glass* at the Philadelphia Museum of Art.

Duchamp's original piece, *The Bride Stripped Bare by Her Bachelors, Even*, most often called *The Large Glass*, was known for the large pane of glass that it featured. When the piece was originally shipped to the museum, Duchamp felt that it was still "incomplete." When the piece arrived at the museum, the large pane of glass had shattered. Duchamp was not upset. He simply declared the piece "complete," telling the museum's curator to mount it as it was. Chance played an important role in all of these artists' works. Learning about art further led me to understand something I had been feeling but couldn't articulate—that what is beautiful in art, as in life, is often defined by the artist and the spectator, but only if you choose to see it so.

On the opening night of *Walkaround Time*, the house was packed. I was busy ushering people to their seats when Marcel Duchamp and his wife, Teeny, walked in, accompanied by a handsome young man whom I did not know. There was a hush in the audience as heads turned to look at them. As I walked them to their seats, I felt the glamour and the exclusivity of the art world that they embodied. Just being in their presence crystallized what I had feared: becoming a high school teacher would be a soul-deep compromise that would never satisfy my newly expanded mind and desire for new adventures and experiences.

My exposure to the avant-garde changed me. I wanted to step off my prescribed path, spread my wings, and create a bolder life through art. All that I had ever been taught to believe about who I was and what I could be was now totally wavering. I had been indoctrinated to believe that, for women, teaching elementary or secondary school students was the best one could do for a vocation. I decided to defy that limitation. Perhaps I would be a college professor, or maybe something else in the art world.

Maybe it was the music, the dancing, or the art that made possible something that I could see for myself. It was this whirlwind of artistic exposure that convinced me to switch my major from secondary education with a concentration in history to liberal arts with a concentration in art history, which was a very limited program at Buffalo State College. Changing my major to a virtually unheard-of profession for women was risky, but I finally felt ready to embrace differentness and chance the unknown.

·

I was helped along by the times. 1968 was that watershed year that caused a planetary shift in thought, behavior, and attitudes. Suddenly, we were a nation in mourning, reeling from the violent deaths of Martin Luther King Jr. and Robert Kennedy. Ivy League suits and button-down collars morphed into tie-dyed T-shirts and jeans. Men's hair grew long, seemingly overnight. The Vietnam War divided the nation and radicalized us as college campuses became battlegrounds of dissent. Mind-altering drugs changed our consciousness and eased us into testing the new cultural, spiritual, and sexual possibilities. For my friends and me, the old days of wading across floors soaked with beer at fraternity parties were suddenly gone. Instead, we now went to parties where the rooms were infused with marijuana smoke, where the bloodshot eyes of coeds grooving to *Sgt. Pepper's Lonely Hearts Club Band* or Bob Dylan's folksy album *John Wesley Harding* peered through the fog. In the outside world, militants proved themselves by smashing bank windows and setting off bombs. Revolution was in the air.

One night, my group of friends and I went to the University at Buffalo to see a rock band called MC5, an event that left an indelible memory in my mind. The band had come from their hippy commune in Michigan, known as the Hog Farm, along with their friends. The university's large gym was packed to capacity with more than a thousand college students, many of whom, like the band members, were tripping on LSD or mushrooms. The band members, with their long, stringy hair and stoned, glazed eyes looked like leering wild animals leaping around the stage. The white lead singer, Rob Tyner, wore a huge Afro. The band's barefoot girl-friends, with long dresses hanging to the floor and ghostly blue-white complexions, their faces drained from ingesting too much psilocybin, swayed on stage in hypnotic, trance-like movements to the deafening music. Their infants hung haphazardly from pouches slung around their necks, small, innocent heads loosely dangling out, bobbing to their mother's gyrations.

One of the band members starting bellowing orders at the audience: "MOTHERFUCKERS . . . I WANT YOU TO HOLD HANDS."

Bleary-eyed strangers obediently turned to each other and took each other's hands.

"NOW, MOTHERFUCKERS," he continued, "I WANT ALL OF YOU TO TAKE A DEEP BREATH IN."

Astonishingly, we did as we were told.

"NOW EVERYBODY EXHALE," he yelled.

We obeyed.

"NOW INHALE," he yelled again.

After a long pause, he bellowed, "EXHALE . . . INHALE . . . EXHALE . . . INHALE," over and over again. His words were mesmerizing as he drove us into a frenzy of hyperventilation. Doing as he ordered, I felt the gymnasium moving as if it was shifting on its axis. We had become one living, breathing embryo swaying side to side in a hallucinatory daze. It seemed like it went on for an eternity.

The spell was finally broken when someone threw a chair. As it crashed into the bleachers, others followed suit, throwing whatever wasn't nailed to the ground. MC5's music could no longer be heard over the mayhem that ensued. Chaos descended as chairs flew through the air, loudly colliding with the metal bleachers and the hardwood gymnasium floor.

I was witnessing anarchy. I saw a young man across the room hit in the head with a wooden chair. With blood dripping from his forehead, he didn't stop throwing chairs, but for me the spell was broken. It was obvious that the world as I knew it had irrefutably changed. After 1968, many young people started questioning and challenging everything about the previous generation's values, the first wave of a tsunami washing away the established ways of thinking about who we were and who we should become. We could no longer travel the narrow pathways previously constructed for us. It left too many of us out.

•

My father died the summer between my junior and senior years of college. At the time, my mother, my brother, and I were crammed into my mother's one-bedroom apartment in Queens. Michael was finished with the military; he slept on the couch in the living room. My mother and I still slept next to each other in single beds in the bedroom.

At 6:00 A.M. on August 3, 1968, the phone rang. It was my Aunt Mary, my father's sister, calling to speak to my mother, so I handed her the phone. In our collective grogginess, we were disoriented by the early call. I could hear my Aunt Mary's mumbled voice through the phone and then my mother hung up. She said only three words: "Max is dead." Not "your father is dead" but "Max is dead," as if she was talking to herself. No tears, no emotion. My brother heard my mother from the living room and his primal scream shook me out of my stupor. I was surprised by his reaction and equally alarmed at my lack of one. I was too stunned to believe that Max Cohen was no longer alive. My pain was beyond tears or outbursts. Numb, I stayed quiet and calm, not knowing what to do with this news. I hadn't spoken to him in three months, angered by his lack of financial support and the hardship he was putting us through. My mother still harbored desperate contempt for him and Michael still harbored fear and rage and hadn't spoken to him in more than six months. We were all left without any closure.

My father was only forty-six years old but had always predicted that he would die from a heart attack, which he spent a lifetime fearing. The night of his death, he had gone to the hospital to see the birth of his second child, a boy, with his former mistress and now wife. When he returned home that night he went to sleep and never woke up. I think my aunt identified my father's body and made the funeral arrangements. His bereaved wife came directly from the hospital to the funeral, still wearing the hospital band on her wrist. My mother, brother, and I went to the funeral home, but only my brother and I attended the funeral. My mother's presence at the home, a few feet away from his new wife, was awkward for everyone, but her need to be there, not only to support her children but also to say good-bye to the man she had been married to for over twenty-three years and only divorced three years before, was understandable. To this day, I have two half brothers I barely know.

It took another year for me to cry. It happened at the unveiling, the customary Jewish ritual of placing the tombstone at the cemetery after a yearlong grieving process, symbolizing that we never forget the person who is gone. By then, I think I was finally ready to release the pain of all that hadn't happened between my father and me, and I fell apart, inconsolable and staggered by my own reaction. I had never fully expressed my longing for a relationship with my father when he was alive. I was too young.

I never got to celebrate the parts of my father that I admired. There had only been time for fear. He will never know that I still reflexively jump when I hear a sudden loud noise in a movie or on the street, or that the fear he instilled in me ricocheted off so many of the men I encountered in my life. He will never know that fear still grips me. He will never know how larger-than-life he was to me, or the fun we could have had together once I was old enough to know him as an adult and put him in his place. I was never able to tell him that.

At the unveiling ceremony, I held on to my fondest memory of him: dancing at the Copacabana, singing to "I Can't Help Myself (Sugar Pie, Honey Bunch)." He will never know, because I never told him, that I loved him.

4

Awakening

It was 1969, the end of a tumultuous decade. Every day, the headlines were crowded with news of Vietnam war atrocities, curiosities, and change. The Manson murders had jolted me, along with much of America. To every media outlet that would listen to them, the perpetrators of these crimes confessed, "We wanted to commit a crime that would shake up the world."

The deaths of Robert Kennedy and Martin Luther King Jr. and the war in Vietnam incited me and others, many of whom were also first-generation college students. We were taught in our classes and in meetings on campus about the history of Vietnam, and we learned to question the lies perpetrated by our government about their reasons for carrying on the war. My female friends and I sat on pins and needles as our male friends waited to be drafted into that hopeless quagmire. We watched the horrors inflicted on our soldiers and the Vietnamese people, which were being televised for the first time.

My search for meaning and my place in the firmament was always ongoing. The only answer that offered me a modicum of peace came from one of my college professors, who said that there was no self, no real stasis of identity, because people were always changing. He said, "To ask the question 'who am I' is to ask a question that has no answer. It takes real courage to live life knowing that." Regardless, I was always searching for answers and understanding and the pursuit was often tormenting.

FIG. 9. Adrienne and me at a Martin Luther King protest march in Buffalo, New York, in 1968, after his assassination.

In reaction to the Vietnam wartime upheavals, the hypocrisies of our parents' generation (which focused so much on materialism and repressive gender roles), and looking for more meaningful and honest ways to live our lives, many young people my age supported artistic expression, experimental drugs, spiritual transcendence, harmony with nature, and communal living. Pants became flared and baggy, colors grew saturated, and patterns such as paisley and mandalas were inescapable, influenced by the new interest in Eastern philosophy and psychedelics. I tripped on mescaline and acid, I sang Hare Krishna mantras with the hippies in Tompkins Square Park, I sat zazen at a Buddhist retreat high in the mountains outside Carmel, California, in the summer of 1969 after my college graduation, and I protested the war.

But I was still determined to climb the career ladder. I was more interested in building my resume than in partaking in political or social groups that would divert me from that goal of self-sufficiency. The motto of the hippies was peace and love, but I never quite believed in the dream that the world would ever fully change from its warmongering past. And although I experimented with hallucinogens as an adventure in experiencing the spiritual unknown, I never fully "turned on to tune out" from my desire to find a way to make a living and take care of myself.

One thing that happened in 1969 that had a huge impact on my later life, even though I was barely aware of it at the time, was the Stonewall riot in New York City. In the early hours of June 28, 1969, police raided the Stonewall Inn, a gay nightclub in Greenwich Village, and a melee ensued as people at the club finally fought back against the police harassment they regularly experienced; thirteen people were arrested. Word spread, and the next day hundreds of gay people gathered to protest the police crackdown and advocate for the legalization of gay bars. Further protests erupted, and on July 27, a group of activists organized the first gay and lesbian march, from Washington Square to the Stonewall Inn.

The Stonewall riot was the tipping point for the gay and lesbian community in New York City and is commonly thought of as the event through which the modern gay rights movement was born. Over the years, thousands of gay men and women across the country had been publicly humiliated, physically harassed, fired, jailed, or institutionalized for being homosexual. In the 1950s and 1960s, the Federal Bureau of Investigation (FBI) and local police departments around the country kept lists of known homosexuals, their friends, and the establishments they frequented. Even the United States Postal Service kept track of addresses where media and materials pertaining to homosexuality were received.[1] College professors merely suspected of being homosexual were fired. Major cities across the country performed sweeps to rid neighborhoods, parks, bars, and beaches of gay people.[2]

Police raids occurred often in bars rumored to cater to homosexuals. During a typical raid, the lights were turned on, customers lined up, and their identification cards checked. Those without identification or dressed in full drag were arrested while the others were allowed to leave with the understanding that they shouldn't show up in bars like these in the future. It was even against the law to *wear clothing* designed for the opposite gender. New York's "Three-Piece Rule" required women to wear three pieces of feminine clothing at all times or else be arrested. Employees and managers of gay bars were often arrested as well.[3]

While no formal laws were in place that prohibited bars from serving liquor to homosexuals, courts granted the New York State Liquor Authority (SLA) broad discretion in approving and revoking liquor licenses for businesses that might become "disorderly." The SLA had the freedom to refer to homosexual activity (visible cross-dressing, same-sex dancing or kissing) as "disorderly." Gay bars were effectively illegal.[4] These strict guidelines left the gay bar industry in the hands of the Mafia, who had the power to operate their clubs without obtaining official liquor licenses. These gangsters had developed a kickback system to pay the police to look the other way. These facts were barely known to me at the time because they were scarcely publicized and I was not involved in any way. They would become apparent and more meaningful to me over time.

New York City's Stonewall uprising in 1969 was the most widely known, although not the only, event to kick-start the gay liberation movement. It was a turning point in the struggle to politicize and empower gays and lesbians that grew out of the civil rights movement and coincided with the revolutionary attitudes of that time.

•

It was during that June month of the Stonewall uprising in 1969 that I graduated from Buffalo State and returned to Queens to share my mother's one-bedroom apartment. It was the only way that I could afford to pursue a master's degree in art history at Queens College. I didn't mind living at home because my mother never curtailed my freedom and we had always enjoyed each other's company. With my father gone, I was able to pay for graduate school with financial aid from both the government and Queens College as well as savings from my summer job working as a receptionist at a men's health club in the city. (I even dated Mr. Universe!) One

FIG. 10. Mom and me at Buffalo State College graduation, 1969.

of the requirements for my financial aid package for graduate school was that I serve as an assistant to one of my professors.

The professor that I worked with changed the trajectory of my personal and professional life. His name was Dr. Robert Pincus-Witten. In addition to working as a professor, he was a well-known art critic and the associate editor of *Artforum* magazine, the most influential contemporary art magazine of the time. We laughed together hard and often as I took dictation for his many articles that were published in *Artforum* and elsewhere. I was astonished by Robert's brilliance. I had never met anyone like him before. He dictated full-length articles off the top of his head with encyclopedic knowledge and a vocabulary of words that I never even knew existed. Furiously, I scratched away in longhand, trying to keep up with the incredible, sometimes obscure, historical connections he made between art and history. Just being in his presence was an education, an awakening that expanded my vision of the world. Suddenly, I was glimpsing his reality—an intellectual and elegant world of wealth and status I hadn't known before.

FIG. 11. My friends at Buffalo State College on graduation day, from left to right: Marcie, Dotty, Adrienne, me, and Dana, 1969.

Robert was gay, but it was never an issue that we discussed openly, at least until much later, simply because at that point in time it did not play any role in our working relationship. Robert never expressed any interest in the burgeoning gay movement because it was so new and not part of his milieu. Art history and writing were his world and he didn't care about political movements unless they were related in some way to his historical perspective about art. Besides, I was dating a lot of men at the time and had no reason to connect with the gay community or their history, including the recent Stonewall uprising.

When I wasn't working with Robert on transcribing his various articles, I was struggling with the demands of the scholarly work I was expected to produce. One of the requirements for my degree was being able to speak or read two languages other than English. I chose Italian and German. When the faculty administration posted the final grades for the language requirement, the list showed the name of each student with a remark beside it. Generally, the remark was "Good."

When I saw my final grade posted on the board, this is what it looked like:

STUDENT 1: Good.
STUDENT 2: Good.
STUDENT 3: Good.
LESLIE COHEN: Good *enough*.

Academically, graduate school was a rude awakening for someone who had skated through her undergraduate education, and I was increasingly frustrated by the heavy workload. Perhaps my undergraduate experience had made me smug, memorizing only what was expected and regurgitating it back with little effort. It was shocking and humbling to discover how little I was prepared for the rigors of graduate school compared to the other students who had arrived with a much more advanced knowledge of art history. I was still so undefined and insecure. These challenges caused me tremendous anxiety as I struggled to keep up and overcome my limitations.

I almost quit. If it weren't for Robert, I would have. In his unforgettable voice with its inimitable Oxford-tinged accent (although he grew up as Bobby Pincus in the Bronx), I can still hear his words: "Whatever you do, you must complete this program. It's a matter of completing what you started rather than what you will ultimately do with the degree. This decision will follow you for the rest of your life."

I am still amazed that Robert was not only my mentor, role model, advocate, and employer but also, eventually, my friend. Not

FIG. 12. Robert Pincus-Witten and me, 2016, at a restaurant in New York City, still friends and laughing as always.

only did he invite me to his highly sophisticated art- and antique-filled country house, which he owned with his longtime partner, Leon, he actually came to dinner at my mother's apartment and ate her humble meatballs and spaghetti. I'll never forget how gracious he was to accept the invitation.

I often wondered what drew such a cultured and urbane man like Robert to me. Was it that he, too, was Jewish, or that he had a mother that he adored as much as I adored mine? Did he know how much I wanted to make my mother proud of me? Did he have that relationship with his mother? Did he relate to me because he grew up a descendant of immigrants from Europe, like my family? Was he also a child with an absentee father and limited financial resources? What made him extend himself like that to me? One thing I do know. He never let his refined sophistication get in the way of his heart. I will remain forever indebted to him for that.

•

Entertaining new ideas about sexual freedom from my art studies and the liberating spirit of the times, I was finally prepared to explore my own tenuous sexuality. I was so sexually immature. I wanted to understand why my friends were having relationships with men and I was not. Sex and intimacy came so naturally to them, while for me it was stressful, like an obligation that I couldn't fulfill. It bothered me because I felt like the odd girl out and I wondered what was wrong with me. I didn't know—or wasn't ready to acknowledge—that I was gay and blamed my inability to connect emotionally with men on my difficult relationship with my father. I did lose my virginity to a man I was very attracted to in my sophomore year of college, but I did not feel comfortable or confident enough to have a deeper relationship with him or other sexual experiences with men after that.

To help me puzzle through my confusion, in early 1970 I found a therapist in Manhattan, whose office was across from Carnegie Hall on 57th Street and who worked on a sliding scale. I rode the subway there from Queens once a week for therapy. In his small office, I revealed all that I could about my childhood, my father, and my deep discomfort with men and their sexuality. I told him that whenever I dated men, I never felt like I could be myself. I confessed that on dates I was often uncomfortable and intimidated and felt the men usurping my power as I became more passive and uncommunicative.

The doctor listened intently to my revelations and then said, "Leslie, what you need to do is to have sex with men."

"What about love and romance and marriage?" I blurted out. Marriage wasn't something that I necessarily wanted, but it was certainly what I was raised to believe that I *should* want, especially before having intercourse. I could only respond to his statement with a stuttering parade of questions: "Really? Which men? How many?"

He responded with a knowing smile. "Yes, really . . . as many as you want." He waited for that to sink in and added, "And, Leslie you don't have to be in love with them to sleep with them . . ."

"I don't?" I interrupted him.

"No, you don't. From what I'm hearing, you just need to get comfortable with your body and get in touch with what satisfies *you*, sexually. If you wait for love, you'll never have sex."

The end of the session was a blur. All I knew was that my therapist had just given me the go-ahead to address my sexual needs, regardless of the constraints of my upbringing. He had given me permission to embark on a sexual journey, which would answer the impossible questions that had weighed me down for as long as I could remember.

I left his office with my mind reeling. I went across the street to the corner newsstand to buy a pack of cigarettes and clear my head. My mind swirled with questions: Who could I have sex with? Who would I pursue? What if I wasn't attracted to anyone? What kind of men was I attracted to? *What kind of man?*

After paying for my cigarettes, I lingered at the newsstand, perusing the magazines that lined the wall. My eyes landed on a pile of magazines on the ground. The stack caught my eye because on the cover were some very serious and angry-looking women marching with placards. Their handmade signs indicated that they were marching for women's rights and protesting the lack thereof. Across the masthead of the magazine was the title, *Notes from the Second Year: Women's Liberation: Major Writings of the Radical Feminists.*[5]

In the lower right quadrant of the magazine was a bullet-point list of feature articles in the issue:

- Love
- The Politics of Housework
- The Left Debate
- Consumerism
- Man Hating
- Consciousness Raising
- The Myth of the Vaginal Orgasm

I bought a copy and shoved it into my bag, eager to get to a private place where I could take it out. I was largely unfamiliar with the burgeoning feminist movement. When I was finally able to dig into the pages, I learned that the publication was created by Shulamith Firestone[6] and other feminists. Much of what I read in *Notes* justified my own long-held yet unconnected beliefs and frustrations. Even though these writings were quite radical and not fully within my sphere of comfort, it was the first time I had seen other women articulate in such a revolutionary fashion my own resentment of how men treated women, and our subjugated and preordained role in society as housewives and lovers.

These protesters were angry at men and I understood. I had gone on enough dates with men to experience how some were so disrespectful as to walk five feet ahead of me, as if they were entitled to be dismissive. It seemed implicit in their behavior that women were subservient. What I experienced with men often felt demeaning, as if I was worth less than they in some unfathomable way.

I had not been introduced to any feminism in college other than as it pertained to the women in the civil rights and antiwar movements who felt pushed aside by men. Even though Betty Friedan's book *The Feminine Mystique* (1963) and her creation of the National Organization of Women (NOW) were instrumental in the start-up of the women's movement, they were not part of my life. By the time I graduated college, women fighting for liberation in the late 1960s and early 1970s were still viewed as radicals and extremists.

Women, for the most part, were still defined by their relation to a man and motherhood. During that first year out of college I was still trying to fit into what was socially expected of me. I was dating a lot of men, as per my therapist's instructions, and struggling to get through my graduate studies. I was still quite bourgeois in many ways, yet change was coming.

Many seminal books written about feminism were first published in 1970 (i.e., "The Dialectic of Sex: The Case for Feminist Revolution," Shulamith Firestone, 1970; "Sexual Politics," Kate Millett, 1970; "Sisterhood Is Powerful," Robin Morgan, 1970; "The Female Eunuch," Germaine Greer, 1970). It was after these books were published that feminist theories began to slowly assimilate through the media to mainstream society. I began to absorb feminist ideas and became even more aware of our shared beliefs through the writings and television appearances of people like Jill Johnston, whose column I read religiously in *The Village Voice*, and Germaine Greer, among others. I thoroughly enjoyed their irreverent attacks on the status quo, heterosexual norms, and patriarchy. At the same time, I was reading about surrealism, Dadaism, and other scandalous art movements of the early twentieth century in my art history courses. These movements were about rejecting cultural norms. I read about female artists and authors living in Paris, including Colette and Anaïs Nin, who both wrote openly about their love affairs with women. I began to fantasize about living a different kind of life, one that was outside the norm, daring, and irreverent.

A fire had been lit. Contemporary women were writing about women's liberation and Sapphic love, from Betty Friedan and Gloria Steinem, the more moderate feminists, to the lesbian feminists Jill Johnston and Valerie Solanas (the woman who shot Andy Warhol in a radical moment of feminist insanity). Although I had no interest in becoming an activist or joining any political groups, all these new ideas about gender, sexuality, and feminism were being absorbed. These artistic women and their unflinching actions, thoughts, and beliefs were seeping into my being with each word that I read, melding together to bolster my inner strength and identity. And through it all, art was pushing me along.

5

Crawling out of Darkness

Four Kent State University students were killed on May 4, 1970, when the National Guard opened fire on a crowd gathered to protest the Vietnam War and the unauthorized invasion of Cambodia. I was on the campus of Queens College when I heard the news and saw groups of students milling together; they were as numbed and disoriented by the broadcast update as I was, shocked, disgusted, and confused by the unnecessary deaths of innocent students by our own government. Soon, more than 450 university, college, and high school campuses across the country were shut down by student strikes and both violent and nonviolent protests that involved more than four million students.

The protests and strikes had a dramatic impact and convinced many Americans, particularly within the administration of President Richard Nixon, that the nation was on the verge of insurrection. I wondered how much more the country could take before it split apart. The air was filled with upheaval. The mobs in New York were smashing windows, slashing tires, dragging parked cars into intersections, even throwing mattresses off overpasses into the traffic down below. Although I did not take part in any of those activities, I sympathized with the uprisings.

Everything was in a state of flux. Like a boiling cauldron, this tumultuous time brought all the discontent, anger, and confusion of people to the surface. I questioned my own behavior, principles, and morals. I was ready to venture out and experiment as I struggled to find my own identity and place within the disorder.

•

I took my doctor's advice and began to have sex with men. It was a big step, but it still wasn't fulfilling. I didn't know how to *be* with men. I never seemed to be able to develop a friendship with them first, before the expectation of sex. Imitating the behavior of other women didn't work. It rarely went well. Being intimate with a man left me feeling uncomfortable and constrained, like I was wearing itchy wool in summer. I struggled to accommodate myself with my perception of how other women behaved with men, and the pretension of ease left me disoriented and wobbly.

One day at school, a fellow art history graduate student, Hannah, invited me to join her and her Swiss boyfriend, Franco, at a party in Greenwich Village. The party was to be held in an impressive penthouse apartment on lower Fifth Avenue overlooking Washington Square Park. I immediately accepted the invitation. Going into "the City" for a party from my mother's apartment in Queens conjured up all kinds of magical fantasies of adventure and wonder.

That night, I planned my outfit very carefully—a black turtleneck sweater, high black leather boots, and a black skirt that went below the knee with a zipper that opened up to the thigh. I wanted to appear as sophisticated and attractive as I could. This was my first taste of cosmopolitan New York nightlife as an adult and I wanted to impress. The night was clear and brisk. As I drove over the Queensborough Bridge into the mouth of the city, I visually embraced the magnificent lights shining from the vast, towering buildings of the city skyline in all their glitter and mystery. Then I made my way downtown.

The party was fairly staid and boring. There was no one there that I really cared about meeting and I felt out of place, even though Hannah and her boyfriend Franco kept me company. The apartment, however, was impressive, with its terrace overlooking Washington Square Park and its incredible sweeping views all the way downtown to Wall Street. *This* was the city I longed to be part of—a city of myriad possibilities.

After the party, Franco and Hannah invited me back to their studio apartment on Charles Street in Greenwich Village for a glass of wine. We drove together in my car, found a parking space, and climbed the stairs to their third-floor apartment. "This is it," Franco said as we entered. "Make yourself at home." As I looked around, I was surprised by how minuscule it was. The kitchen was part of the small hallway to the bathroom. The one room housed only a double bed in one corner pressed up against the wall and a deflated pink plastic blow-up chair crumpled up on the floor in the other corner. There was no place for me to sit other than on the edge of their bed.

While Hannah poured the wine and put on some music, Franco climbed around me on the bed and lay down, propped up against the wall. Hannah handed us each a glass of wine as the sound of an exquisite album of the Argentine mass *Misa Criolla* filled the room. The Spanish language and the choral voices behind them were reverent and like nothing I had ever heard before. The soothing sounds temporarily reduced the tension that was slowly mounting in me.

Hannah lay down on the other side of Franco so that I was sitting on the edge of the bed and Franco and Hannah were lying next to me. The moment felt strange and staged, as if they were preparing me for something. Nervously, I kept up with Hannah's small talk as I watched Franco unwinding on the bed, gently caressing Hannah's arm as she spoke.

"What is your thesis on?" she asked.

"New York Dada and its influence on American art," I answered.

"Interesting . . . Franco and I are thinking about going back to Switzerland to work on my thesis on Puvis de Chavannes. We're talking about it . . ."

"That would be wonderful," I said.

Hannah paused. "Will you excuse me for a moment? I have to use the bathroom."

Hannah lifted herself off the bed. As she walked toward the bathroom, Franco looked at me sitting stiffly on the edge of the bed, patted the bed, and urged, "Leslie, please make yourself more comfortable."

I felt awkward but I told myself that he was just being polite. In order to comply with his request, I leaned against the wall which served as a backboard, leaving my legs dangling off the side of the bed. As more time passed, Hannah had still not come out of the bathroom. I wondered why she was taking such a long time. Was she sick? Should someone go check on her?

Finally, I heard the bathroom door open and Hannah walk back into the room. When I turned to look at her, she was standing there stark naked with her dark eyes locked on mine. Jarred by the sight of her and the intensity in her eyes, I quickly looked away. She walked toward the bed, climbed back into it, and pulled the sheer cotton batik cover over her body.

I was stunned. My mind was a television screen that had lost its picture and was filled with noisy static. Then, after a few more moments, which seemed like an eternity to me, Hannah leaned over Franco and took my hand. My whole body went rigid. I could barely breathe. I pulled my hand away. *What was happening?* Had she reached for my hand simply as a friendly gesture or was it something more? Was she coming on to me or was it all in my head? Finally, not being able to stand the silence any longer, I said, "Look, I don't know what's going on here, but I think I should leave."

Hannah's face reddened and contorted. Tears began to stream down her face.

The needle on the record player had returned to its base. The room was totally silent.

Franco turned to look at me to see if I would change my mind but, not getting the desired response, quickly got off the bed and offered to walk me to my car. As he got his shoes on and quickly tamed his mussed hair, I waited by the door. We walked out of the apartment, down the hall stairs, and outside to the car in complete silence.

When we reached my car and I was about to get in, he said, "I'm sorry." I looked at him, still undone by what had happened, trying to build up my confidence to ask the only question that really mattered. Finally, I said, "Franco, was Hannah coming on to me?"

Franco hesitated. Then, he said, "Yes, she was. She's been interested in you for a long time."

Relieved that I wasn't imagining it, I responded, "thank you for telling me." I offered only an apologetic smile and said good-bye.

I got into the car and, as I drove home, screamed into the darkness like a valve that was opened to let the steam escape. A lifetime of pent-up, repressed sexual energy, sublimated with drugs, drinking, dancing my ass off, breaking rules, and recklessness, was facing the abyss of newfound freedom and it terrified me.

When I arrived home, I sat in the car for a while longer, processing what had just occurred. When I finally calmed down, I sat back and smiled, finally settling into the truth of what I was feeling: fear, anxiety, but mostly excitement. It was like this night had finally presented me with the opportunity to break through to the other side. Like Duchamp's masterpiece, I thought; only when the glass broke was it complete.

·

In the days that followed, I was totally absorbed with analyzing what had happened and how I had reacted. I was twenty-three years old and I had been offered a key to my sexual freedom. Somewhere deep inside, I knew that by discovering my own sexual possibilities, other doors would open—both good and bad. I thought about how fear had contained me in my life and I felt like a coward. Was I all talk? What was I so afraid of? Night after night I asked myself—wasn't I ready to start living life on my own terms? I made a decision. The next time I knew I would not run away.

When I saw Hannah at school, I approached her. "Hi," I said to her, tentatively, not sure how she would react. She seemed surprised that I was approaching her. "Hi," she said back.

"Listen, I'm sorry if I made you uncomfortable the other night. It was my hang-up. It had nothing to do with you. I really would like to get together with you and Franco again sometime."

"Sure, we can do that," she said. After a moment she asked, "How about Friday night?"

"Okay," I said. "What time?"

"8:00 p.m.," she said, and she smiled and walked away.

·

The night that Hannah and I made love, it was Franco's lovemaking that eased me into accepting Hannah's kisses. I enjoyed making love with Franco but the intimacy with Hannah was very awkward at first. It was foreign to me to feel her softness and strange to have a woman touch my breasts and for me to caress hers. I was uncomfortable. But soon I felt a melding, an ease and familiarity with her body, and her reactions to my touch empowered me. I had never before had that sense of sexual fortitude with a man. Afterwards, I thought that maybe, in some way, being with women could rectify the loss of power I felt around men. Maybe, through women and my own self-emancipation, I would enter the world of passion and desire that I had craved and dreamed of, but that had eluded me. I knew that this experience with Hannah and Franco was not the end but the beginning of an exploration of myself.

·

Shortly thereafter, Hannah told me she was going to Europe with Franco to write her graduate thesis and asked me if I wanted to stay in their apartment while they were away. I jumped at the opportunity, happily moving out of my mother's apartment. I was ecstatic about living on my own in the city. Ever since I was a young girl, Manhattan represented myriad dreams of intoxicating freedom, career achievement, and untold adventures.

Another art history graduate student from Queens College, John, lived just a few blocks away on Cornelia Street, and we started to meet up regularly. John revealed to me that he was gay, and I confided in him about my single experience with Hannah and Franco. We became immediate buddies. Having just moved into the big city, it was comforting to have a friend living right around the corner.

Handsome, smart, and engaging, John introduced me to the allures of the big city. Every chance we had, John and I walked the streets of Greenwich Village, perusing antique stores on Bleecker Street and cruising beautiful men as they walked along Christopher Street. (I still rationalized that I was straight; that I had had a lesbian *experience*.) We looked into store windows and people watched endlessly. We talked about relationships, careers, school, and our dreams for the future. He introduced me to his world of gay men. He told me about his gay escapades, including his trips to bathhouses and his preference for anonymous sex. New York was the art capital of the world and, as budding art historians, we could not get enough. We were the perfect culture vulture pair—devouring art, theater, and dance happenings around town.

One night, John took me to a party at his friends David and Manuel's downtown loft on Canal Street. It was before Soho became gentrified, so the neighborhood was still rough and edgy, filled with discount supply stores whose wares flowed over onto the street. Canal Street was jammed with people doing business during the day but desolate at night. As instructed, when we arrived, we called from a pay phone inside the topless bar a few doors down from their loft building to let them know we were there. Then we walked back to their building and they threw the keys down from their third-floor window so we could let ourselves in. We took the large, clanking industrial lift up to their floor, where the elevator door opened directly into their large, art-filled loft space. I had brought a bunch of peacock feathers as a gift, the poor man's bouquet commonly sold in every newsstand around the city at the time. The elegance of calla lilies or anemones would have been much more their style, but how was I to know? I was so wet behind the ears I was leaving puddles at my feet.

When I saw Manuel, I could not believe my eyes. He was the same beautiful young man that I had seated with Marcel and Teeny Duchamp at Merce Cunningham's dance premiere at Buffalo State College back in 1968! And now here I was with him and his friends in his loft. David was an artist and Manuel was an assistant at the prominent Sidney Janis gallery, which represented some of the leading artists of the time like Claes Oldenburg, Ellsworth Kelly, and George Segal.

That night, the sculptor Marisol Escobar was there with Teeny Duchamp, the widow of the late, great Marcel Duchamp, who had died in October 1968. Teeny had also been married to a member of the Matisse family. Here I was, the borough bumpkin, sitting across from art royalty, trying very hard not to let my total lack of sophistication show. My naïveté must not have been too much of an impediment because, soon after that first meeting, David and Manuel took me in and I became part of their elite circle of friends. Whenever I went to their home, I met someone from the art world who I had studied or read about.

•

When Hannah returned from Europe, I had to give the apartment back to her. Because I had now lived "in the City," there was absolutely no way I was going back to my mother's apartment in Queens. I had another opportunity to sublet an apartment for three months from an art history friend who was going to Europe to do research for her thesis. It was a one-bedroom walk-up apartment on the sixth floor of a tenement building on East 69th Street that cost ninety dollars a month, but I needed a roommate to split the rent with.

My cousin Ellen and I were still very close. She and her husband, Howie, who was one of my best friends from high school (I had introduced them), were living in the city at the time. Ellen introduced me to her friend Suri from graduate school who was also looking for an apartment. We didn't know each other well but immediately took to one another. She agreed to move in and split the rent with me. She was a very attractive woman with blonde hair and crystal-blue eyes who was studying, as was my cousin Ellen, to become a psychologist.

The place we were to share was very small; it didn't even have a sink in the bathroom, so you had to wash and brush your teeth in the kitchen. I slept in the tiny single bedroom that was more like a large closet and Suri slept on the couch in the living room. Suri and I had a lot in common. We were both Jewish girls from the boroughs, graduate students, ambitious and attractive. We enjoyed talking to each other and sharing our lives. It was a good roommate match.

After Hannah returned from Europe, we were sexually together again one or two more times without Franco, who had remained in Europe. I never thought there was any chance of a relationship between Hannah and me other than a sexual one. I really wasn't interested in taking it any further than that. But when I moved into the new apartment with Suri, it turned out that Hannah wasn't quite done with me.

The only phone in the apartment was in the living room, where Suri slept, near the doorway to my bedroom. I always slept nude, and one night when Hannah called unexpectedly late, I jumped out of bed, still foggy from sleep, to stop the phone ringing, not wanting it to wake Suri. It was so sudden that I neglected to put anything on. I looked over at Suri's bed to see if she had woken up only to see Suri peering at my naked body. Embarrassed, I quickly got off the phone, apologized for waking her, and went back into my room.

A few nights later, while we were sipping wine and conversing together on the couch, immersed in another of our long discussions about art, life, and love, Suri swerved the conversation over to the topic of bisexuality, which was a hot topic with a lot of progressive young folks at the time.

As she continued talking, I became more and more uncomfortable, fearing that I would reveal too much of myself and scare her. I told myself to stay calm. What kept running through my mind was *if she thinks that you're a lesbian, she'll be uneasy about sharing the apartment with you.*

I wasn't ready for what happened next.

Pointedly, she asked, "Leslie, have you ever slept with a woman?" Her querying eyes peered at me.

I was momentarily silent. I spoke slowly, grudgingly: "Yes. Recently, I had an 'experience' for the first time." I didn't want to go into detail about Hannah, since it was just an "experience."

"I would like to have that 'experience' too," she said.

Trying to appear as unthreatening as possible, I said, "I'm sure you will someday."

Without skipping a beat, Suri looked deeply into my eyes and said, "Leslie, I want to have that experience with you."

As my mind left my body and suspended itself in midair, I stammered, "Oh."

Seeing that I was frozen, after a few more moments, Suri extended her hand and said, "Why don't we just go into the bedroom and lie down together."

I was terribly shy, but I was definitely attracted to Suri, so I took her hand and let her lead me into the bedroom.

·

I was now twenty-four and it was my first love affair—intensely passionate and emotionally eruptive. Suri was an emotional, beautiful, and intelligent woman. I had never felt such desire before. It was the deeply romantic love I had always looked for that had eluded me all those years. Now it was my turn, and love poured out of me like a broken spigot. The way that she responded intensified my passion. The sensation of being open and sexual with someone that I desired and cared so deeply about, for the first time, hit me like a fever, a blaze of sunlight, a kaleidoscope of colors. I was incredibly raw and vulnerable, stripped bare by the intensity of my love. I just wanted to be in bed with her all the time. I was intoxicated by her smell, her skin, her lips, her eyes.

Being with a woman began to feel very natural. Her reactions to my touch freed me to realize my own pure pleasure. It was the first time I was actually relaxed enough to enjoy sex. *This* is what people were talking about! With men, I was always passive, reduced to a mere receptacle. They ran the show. Many of the men I was with back then did not know how to please a woman, and I never knew how to ask for what I wanted. Sex with a woman was sex on an equal playing field. I never understood what passion meant until I was wrapped in a woman's arms.

Although we never called ourselves a couple, it was clear that Suri and I were in love. This was my first adult relationship and the first time I lived with a lover, yet we were so isolated in our own closed-off world. The only people who knew the nature of our relationship were Ellen and Howie. We did not know any other lesbians, at least anyone that admitted it. After we were together for some time, we longed to dance close to each other, to hold each other openly at a nightclub, but we didn't know where to go. In 1971, most of the world still considered our love perverse, but we were determined to find a place to slow dance together where we would not be judged. So we decided to go to Greenwich Village, the bohemian enclave of artists, outsiders, and homosexuals, to search it out.

"How will we know where to go?" Suri asked as we nervously rode the subway downtown to the Village.

"I think we should walk around until we see someone who's obviously gay and then ask them where women hang out."

It wasn't as easy as we had thought it would be. Suri and I circled the Village for what seemed like forever. We walked and watched people of all sizes, shapes, and colors going about their normal business. I'm sure that we passed hundreds of gay people, but neither of us knew for sure or could conjure up the courage to speak to any of them. We walked, talked, peered, and pointed.

We passed the open doors of the music clubs that were sprinkled throughout the streets of the West Village. Every time we walked by one of them, we were enveloped by the seductive jazz, folk, and rock melodies that wafted out into the streets. The music pouring out of those doors reminded me of standing with my mother outside the Metropole in Times Square, hearing the sounds of the percussionist, Mongo Santamaría, and memories of Beth and me hearing the music from the street before entering and dancing together in that dark nightclub in downtown Buffalo.

That night, our search for gays turned into a game, discreetly eyeing people to see if we could decipher their sexuality.

"Look at his walk. He must be," I said.

"You think?" Suri said.

"Maybe," I whispered.

It was futile. We couldn't know for sure and we were too nervous to approach anyone.

"How do you go up to a stranger to ask if they're gay, anyway?" Suri said.

"We can't. It's too weird," I replied with frustration.

Then I remembered that I had recently read an interesting article in *The Village Voice* on the new gay movement that was developing, which mentioned a lesbian political organization called Daughters of Bilitis (DOB). From a phone booth, I looked up their number and called. When someone answered, I nervously asked: "Can you tell me where I can find a lesbian club?"

"No, I'm sorry, we do not divulge that kind of information."

I was disheartened to hear the response and needed to understand. "Why is that?" I asked, annoyed.

"We do not support those kinds of clubs," the woman said and hung up.

"Those kinds of clubs?" I didn't understand. If not *them*, who, then, could help us? Where were we supposed to go? A few years later, I finally understood why they wouldn't divulge the names of "those kinds of clubs." The Mafia ran the lesbian clubs in New York City, and DOB did not want to support the Mafia, but that did not help us when we were desperately trying to find someplace that welcomed us.

Suri and I were getting nowhere and about to give up. Tired and hungry, we finally stopped at a neighborhood diner on Eighth Avenue for something to eat. As soon as the extremely effeminate waiter sashayed over to our table, it was apparent that he was about as queer as you could be. This was our opportunity. Suri and I winked at each other and, in a whisper, I timidly asked him if he knew where we could find a lesbian club.

He responded with ease. "Sure. Cooky's—it's not far from here."

Just posing the question and getting the answer took so much out of us that we simply nodded our heads like robots without asking him anything else. After we ate, we ran out of the restaurant to get the address from the phone book at the corner pay phone. Within minutes, we had an address and hailed a cab to get there.

The cab ride seemed to take forever. As we headed farther and farther north, we were bewildered but determined to find this club. It dawned on me that we might have the wrong address. The waiter had said that Cooky's was close to where we were but we were now approaching Harlem.

Eventually, the taxi pulled over and the driver said, "Ladies, this is as far as I go. The address you want is just a few blocks further east, but you'll have to walk the rest of the way."

I said, "What do you mean, walk? Can't you take us there?"

The driver said, "No. You'll see why . . . it's just around the corner, so it's not far. Make a right and you'll find it."

We paid him and started to walk toward Cooky's.

As soon as we reached the dilapidated building that housed "Cooky's," we knew we had made a huge mistake. This clearly was not the club we were looking for. We were in the belly of Harlem and Black women and men were going in and out of the club. This was *not* a lesbian bar. It was a dive with derelicts out front. Looking around, we understood why the cabbie wouldn't take us any farther than he had. Danger lurked everywhere. What we read as menacing Black and brown faces surrounded us, staring and wondering how we got there. There were no smiles and no welcoming gestures. On the street, there were no cars, buses, or taxis. Strung out people—drug dealers, hookers, and junkies—were everywhere, milling around in the middle of the road or in doorways of tenement buildings.

Here we were, looking for our first lesbian bar and, instead, stuck in the heart of an unknown world of sinister, desolate characters that looked nothing like us. It was like we were in some sort of modern-day Hieronymus Bosch painting. Suri's blonde hair and big blue eyes could not be missed. We stood out like a pair of headlights passing through a dark tunnel. There was a cacophony of sounds emanating through the sullen night air. Men and women hung out of tenement windows, yelling down at their customers and johns. Loud laughter and screams sounded in the distance. The noise of senseless chatter from the mouths of strung-out junkies bounced from corner to corner and stoop to stoop. It felt like hundreds of eyeballs peered at us as if we were potential prey. We were terrified.

We had exhausted our cash on the long cab ride uptown, so could not afford another taxi ride home. We stood on the corner, searching for a way out of there. We so wanted not to be afraid because Suri and I were your typical, liberal, college-educated white girls—holding picket signs high in college, marching against the inequality of the races, earnestly wanting to feel connected to the plight of Black people. I had marched for civil rights on 125th Street in Harlem when I was still in high school and again in college. But this was not 125th Street. This was a scene I had never before experienced.

Without seeing a bus stop anywhere and feeling trapped and panicked, we decided to take our chances and approached three men standing together on the corner. Trying to keep my voice from shaking, I said, "Excuse me. Can you tell us where we can find a bus stop?"

The men looked at one another and then the tallest one said, "Sure. It's a walk. But, if you want, we'll take you there."

All people are inherently good was our liberal white girl motto and, with that in mind, we agreed to walk with them, hoping we could trust them. As we walked and time passed, we began to feel more secure. We made small talk, and a kind of camaraderie formed between us. The bus stop was a distance away but we were feeling relatively safe now that these men were with us. A short time later, they stopped and turned to us.

"Ladies, if you don't mind, we need to make a pit stop to pick up some *cheeba cheeba*," one of them said.

We didn't know what *cheeba cheeba* was, but, not wanting to look vulnerable and stupid, we played along. When we reached the building, the short one asked, "Wanna go up with us? It won't take long."

"No, thank you. We'll wait here."

The tall one said to his friends, "I'll stay here and watch out for them."

The other two men then disappeared into the apartment building. After they scored the *cheeba*, they came back downstairs and we continued walking. "I need something to drink," the short one said as we passed a corner bodega. Once again, we stopped, and they went into the store. We waited outside. Finally, we arrived at the bus stop. We had no idea how long we'd have to wait.

"Ladies, want to smoke some *cheeba* with us while you wait?"

Suri and I looked at each other and, wanting to at least *appear* to feel safe with them and not insult their kindness, we said, "Okay, sure." We followed them into the lobby of a desolate apartment building next to the bus stop. Despite the bare lightbulbs dangling from the ceiling, it was forebodingly dim. It was there, in the complete silence of that vacuous tiled space, that one of the men pulled out a long knife and placed it against the thin straps of my large Moroccan red leather shoulder bag resting against my side. The small mirrors in the bag reflected their faces and the surroundings. With a small jerky motion, he indicated that he would either cut the strap or stab me. It was my choice.

"Give me your money," he said, with a lethal look in his eyes that had suddenly changed from friend to demon.

I looked over at Suri and saw the blood drain from her terrified face. Four dollars was all we had left between us. Trembling, I nervously reached into my bag and handed him four one-dollar bills. That left us with no money for the bus. Frightened but desperate, I asked, "Can you just give us a dollar for the bus?" The thief glared at me for a moment, like I had lost my mind. I did not know whether he was about to kill, beat, or rape us. Then he begrudgingly handed me a dollar bill. In a very cold, ominous voice, he said, "Now, don't say another word."

He looked at his friends and they turned and left us there, shaken but grateful to be alive. With their departure, Suri and I quickly ran to the bus stop and arrived just as the bus appeared in the distance.

•

We eventually did, a couple of weeks later, make it to Kooky's, spelled with a *K*, not with a *C*. It was, like the waiter said, only a few blocks from the diner where he had waited on us. Standing outside of it on West 14th Street, we hesitated. When you have heard all your life that homosexuals are aberrant, disturbed human beings, it's very strange to stand outside a lesbian club on the verge of entering. It is the confrontation with your inner self, the negative information that you have been indoctrinated with all your life banging up against the reality of your deep love and desire for another person of the same sex. There I was at the threshold of before and after.

Anxiously peering through the front window, we were scared. What would we find inside this "well of loneliness"?[1] My mind was filled with preconceived images of rough-and-tumble lesbians, playing the roles of either "butch" or "femme," and it wasn't a pretty picture to me. It seemed unnecessary for someone to have to define themselves by these old-fashioned gender roles that feminism was now resisting.

Finally, we opened the door to the bar and walked in. It was a quiet night and the crowd was sparse. We noticed some butch customers standing around, but there were also women who looked like us and passed for "straight." At the long bar, I spotted a couple, one of whom I think may have been Kooky. She was short and stocky and dressed in a men's suit and tie. All that was missing was the walking cane and monocle worn by the fanciful Parisian lesbians of the 1920s. Leaning on her was her totally "femme" girlfriend, all done up in a short, tight skirt and high heels. She had perfectly coiffed long black hair and manicured red nails and was leaning into her short, paunchy butch lover. Now, in the context of modern-day queer liberation, their role-playing might seem "cool" because, these days, self-determination is sexy. But back then, during the evolution of second wave feminism, the butch-femme roles felt like the continuation of an unwelcome anachronism of role-playing oppression.

After all Suri and I had been through to find this place, though, we felt that the least we could do was have a drink and stay a while. We danced together on a small dance floor in the back of the club. Although we felt as though our mission had been accomplished, since we could hold each other openly, we still felt a bit like aliens. The club was tacky. We didn't belong there. Several women approached us, asking if we were foreigners. In many ways, we were.

We left soon after we finished our drinks. I had no idea that this was just the beginning of my foray into the world of lesbian clubs.

•

Eventually, sex with Suri became a struggle. She pulled back, not nearly as demonstrative or available as I wanted her to be. I was always ready and eager, and her coolness hurt and confused me. I was so in love with her, and I thought she felt the same about me. But after three months, when the sublet was up, she told me that she wanted to find her own place. I was utterly heartbroken and desperate to hold onto her. Why would she leave when she told me she loved me? I did not understand then or for years afterward. I guess the truth was she did not love me enough to want to be in a relationship with a woman. Although Suri enjoyed the emotional and sexual satisfaction that came from being with a woman, I think she still longed for everything that straight life could offer, namely a man who could provide societal acceptance, children, and, in the then predominant worldview, "things as they ought to be."

After we moved out of our apartment, Suri spent another three months living with me at my new apartment on the Upper West Side until she found her own place and was gone. She came back to me in between her boyfriends with false promises of rekindling our romance. Of course, we would have sex. I was too numb to be indignant. For a while, I gave her what she wanted, but I began to feel used and, over time, we saw each other less and less frequently. Our relationship transformed me and broke my heart.

6

Acceptance

After the classwork part of graduate school ended, while I toiled away on my thesis, I worked at a couple of art galleries in the city. My mentor, Robert Pincus-Witten, procured every job I ever had in the art world. Eventually, he introduced me to his very wealthy associate and publisher, Charlie Cowles, whose father had gifted him *Artforum* magazine. Robert told me Charlie was looking for a secretary.

When I interviewed with Charlie at his loft in SoHo, he asked me what I wanted to do at the magazine. I said, "Truthfully, anything but be a secretary." It was a brave move, but it worked. He created a new position for me, general manager, which was a kind of girl Friday job. I did whatever was asked of me by the small staff of five who put out the magazine every month, and my tasks were endless. I did a little bit of everything, including handling back issues, proofreading articles, and setting type. When the magazine subsequently faced dire financial straits and bankruptcy, I found a way to save it thousands of dollars through monitoring its distribution and created, along with the editor John Coplans, and headed *Artforum*'s first circulation and subscription department. All the while, I was working on my graduate thesis.

•

After Suri left, Ellen and Howie moved in with me to help me pay the rent and heal. The breakup with Suri had left me unmoored. Ellen and Howie had an open marriage, and we experimented with the idea of a three-way marriage (which was never sexually consummated on my end). That period was a crazy time for us and our new group of friends, as we challenged every societal taboo and rule presented to us. We intentionally tore the fabric of society apart to see what would be left. Upturning everything we were ever taught about how we were supposed to live our lives was dangerous because we also chipped away at and eroded the very foundations that moored us.

Our small group of friends included dancers and writers who would come in and out of our apartment at all hours. We went clubbing. Drugs muted our consciousness. Night became day and day became night. The only structure I had was the walk I made every morning across Central Park from the Upper West Side to my job at *Artforum* on Madison Avenue. It gave me the opportunity to soak up nature, and the quiet surroundings stabilized me for my daytime job. As we became more and more untethered, old, unresolved wounds simmered up to the surface through the cracks of our relationships. Howie and Ellen's marriage fell apart, and eventually Howie moved out. Ellen remained for another few months.

Trying to hold myself together, I visited a new, female therapist, who told me that she wouldn't be able to work with me because I was bisexual. It's hard to believe in retrospect that a therapist would refuse to treat you for being attracted to your own sex, especially since homosexuality at that time was considered by the psychiatric profession to be a psychosis. You would think that, since her profession considered me mentally ill, she would consider it her responsibility to treat me.[1] It shocked and angered me that she refused because I was still getting comfortable with acknowledging my own sexuality, and I thought the therapist's reaction was not only deplorable but alarmingly unprofessional. To be rejected for being who I was was an emotional setback that I believe manifested itself in another disturbing incident that occurred shortly thereafter.

One night, while I was alone in the apartment and Ellen was out on a date, I was lying in bed, watching television. I turned off the television to go to sleep when, suddenly, I saw a large, ghostly light suspended in the air in front of me. Petrified, I was sure that it was my dead father's spirit. A lightning bolt of terror, like a power surge, passed through my entire body from head to toe. The massive onslaught of fear that was so ingrained in me from all those years of living with him was so intense that my limbs froze and I could not speak. I couldn't grasp what I was seeing or what was happening. I lay on the bed, paralyzed from head to foot. All I could feel was the furious beat of my heart and the tears running down my face.

I remained there, unable to move, helpless in the dark for what seemed like an eternity, whimpering to myself until I finally heard the apartment door open. I somehow managed to scream out, "ELLEN!" She ran into the room. When she saw the sheer panic in my eyes, she knew what to do. She sat down beside me on the bed, stroked me gently, talked softly to me, loving and patient, and soothed me back to myself. I will never forget her words because she said exactly the right thing: "Don't worry, my love. Wherever you are going, I am going with you." If I was going mad, she would go there with me. I was not alone. Her love brought me back to sanity.

·

When my love affair with Suri ended, I mourned and sulked for a year and then, strangely, the veil lifted, and I was free—liberated in a way I had never before experienced. I no longer felt shame about being gay. Accepting my sexuality helped unleash me from society's constraints of gender and role-playing and both defined and emboldened me. I had not felt this kind of empowerment and sense of freedom since I was a prepubescent girl playing stickball back in the parking lot in Queens. I was finally ready to direct my own life.

No longer afraid of my lesbianism, my social circle widened, and I met some other lesbians. Suri still lingered in my life as an occasional tryst, but as time went on, she faded further and further into the background. Making up for lost time, I took lovers, both male and female, and entered full steam ahead into the land of multiple possibilities. "Come home with me . . . just for the night. . . ." I just wanted to experience it all without the commitment. I wanted to fly in every way I could, unencumbered. But, in between my rigorous job at *Artforum* and my various liaisons, I was stretched thin. I started to be more reflective about what I was doing and what I really wanted for my life. I needed to make some choices.

Through dating both men and women, I came to the conclusion that women offered me more. I sensed that most men would override my wishes with their sense of entitlement, aggressiveness, and arrogance. With women, I had more of an opportunity to decipher who I was and what I wanted. I did not have to expend my energy futilely trying to please a man. Also, I was sexually empowered with women. After all, before men became more aware of a woman's physiognomy because of feminism, few men knew or cared to learn how to physically please women. I, on the other hand, had mastered a woman's body and flourished as a lover. With women, I felt sexually unfettered. I accepted myself as an outsider in the society at large, but as an insider in the very exclusive club of women that included the legendary and creative lesbians or bisexuals that I had been studying and reading about for years. I celebrated, because they would be the women's shoulders on which I would proudly stand.

The knowledge that I couldn't live a conventional life because of who I truly was undeniable. Feeling confident about who I was meant that there would no more struggling and straddling the fence. As my first therapist suggested, after experiencing sex, I could freely embrace my own desires. Those mostly hollow trysts with men were simply a gauge to measure where I was on the sexuality spectrum. I was definitely on my way to becoming a full-fledged lesbian. I flourished in the company of women. I always had.

•

How did I first meet other lesbians? During those outrageous times when Howie and Ellen and I all lived together and friends gathered at our apartment, I met a woman named Helene through a mutual friend, and she became my first lesbian friend. She was a beautiful, outrageous writer, part-time sex worker, and former premed student. Helene and I cared deeply for each other and shared a love of lesbian literary figures, especially Gertrude Stein and Alice B. Toklas. I was attracted to her, but our coupling was not meant to be. We slept together once, more out of a sense of lesbian obligation than desire, but the lovemaking felt mechanized, like I was one of her paying customers. After that, our friendship remained platonic, but Helene, being possessive of my attention, never introduced me to other lesbians.

A few months later, when Helene's on-again, off-again girlfriend, Diane, asked me if I could host a party for Helene's birthday at my large apartment, I jumped at the opportunity so that I could meet other women. On the night of the party, my apartment was filled with lesbians. With my newfound acceptance of myself and after meeting other lesbians for the first time, I was in all my glory.

One of the guests, Michelle Florea, took to me immediately. She was very funny, with a strong, assertive personality. We hit it off. A few weeks later, I was out with Helene at a lesbian club called the Lib and ran into Michelle, who spotted me from across the room.

She came over to me and said, "Hi. Good to see you again."

"Good to see you, too," I said. "How are you doing?"

"Fine." She then leaned in and whispered in my ear, playfully, "Hey, listen, some friends and I are going to have an orgy later. Want to come?"

I looked straight into her eyes and called her bluff. "Sure."

She was taken aback, not only because she was really only kidding and did not expect me to say yes but also because she had never been in an orgy before and now she had to make one happen. Little did she know, when she facetiously asked me, that I was game for anything. To hell with Suri's circumlocutions and my moping; to hell with society's containment and rules; to hell with the idea of finding my one "true" love. I was over it all.

Meanwhile Michelle, from the time she met me at Helene's birthday party, had decided that her previous romance was over and that instead she wanted a relationship with me. She pursued me with a determination that was hard to put off. Nothing stopped her. In those days, she was an anomaly among the women I knew, with an aggressiveness that was unusual. After being immersed in academia and the art world, this was the first time that I had met a wheeler-dealer woman with street smarts, and I was impressed and intrigued by her fearlessness and independence. As I got to know her over time, I realized that she could also be highly defensive; she compensated for her insecurities through the use of bravado, combativeness, and especially humor. She was one of the funniest people I have ever met.

As I stated before, my sexual exploration with men and women at that time was celebratory but, regardless of all the fun I was having, I was also exhausted. In the end, I had *too many* lovers and not enough time. I needed to find a balance. It became clear that I should settle down with Michelle. Or, to put it more succinctly, Michelle decided to settle down with me and she persisted until she got what she wanted. Before I could give living together any more thought, Michelle's clothes were hanging in my closet.

I was reluctant to live with a girlfriend. I was still a newborn bursting out of my closet, and I wanted to explore what I had missed, like someone who'd been denied food for too long and then presented with a pupu platter. I warned Michelle in advance that I did not want to be monogamous so, perhaps naively, she agreed to an open relationship. As a result, Michelle and I shared sexual partners like Chinese combo dinners—one from Group A, two from Group B, or some variation thereof. We were young and impulsive, with a limited grasp of the consequences of playing around.

My cavorting ended after a while. The fun was over. How many times can you ride the roller coaster before the thrill wears thin and even becomes tiresome? Faces detach from bodies, bodies from beating hearts. The excitement and pleasure dull, just bounce off the surface, like a rock you've skimmed across the water that grazes the top but never goes deeper. The "scenes" became boring.

•

Michelle, intrigued by my travel stories, wanted to travel around Europe, which she had never done. She made me promise that after my thesis was complete, I would quit my job at *Artforum* and go to Europe with her. In 1973, I finally finished my thesis and kept my promise to Michelle. I was still only earning $7,000 a year at *Artforum*. You read that right, *not* a month, a *year*. New York City was very inexpensive in those days, but I was ready to move on.

After about two months abroad, spent mostly on the island of Rhodes in Greece, we returned to the States. I needed to reconnect with the art world and find a job. Michelle and I moved into an apartment on lower Fifth Avenue. After a few months, Robert connected me to Mario Amaya, the director of the New York Cultural Center, an innovative museum that operated as a *kunsthalle* (i.e., a museum without a permanent collection), with the ability to mount shows that were both innovative and unique. Mario was looking to hire an associate curator, a job that would be a huge step up for me in my career. In June 1974, with Robert's strong recommendation and my interview, I was hired.

Mario Amaya, a legend in the art world, was known for his scholarship, drug abuse, and sexual escapades. He was also famous for, unfortunately, being shot, along with Andy Warhol, by Valerie Solanas. Luckily, his wounds were not as serious as Warhol's. He was gay, flamboyant, and very handsome. He was also incredibly promiscuous and dysfunctional.

Often, he wouldn't show up at work, forcing me to step in and take on the enormous responsibilities of running a museum with a large staff and exhibition schedule. I was in charge of everything in his absence. It was an incredibly high-maintenance task to work for him. Watching his moods swing from hysterical to nasty to charming to brilliant all within the same day was grueling and, when he was incapacitated for one reason or another, I was left with a lot to handle, including fixing his mess-ups.

This was the most exhausting, challenging, and exciting period of my life. Through this life-altering job and my relationship with Mario, I met a lot of famous artists, writers, and culturati, rich people who lived in fancy Park Avenue apartments with walls covered in silk damask and the paintings of Matisse and Picasso. I attended small dinner parties with Norman Mailer

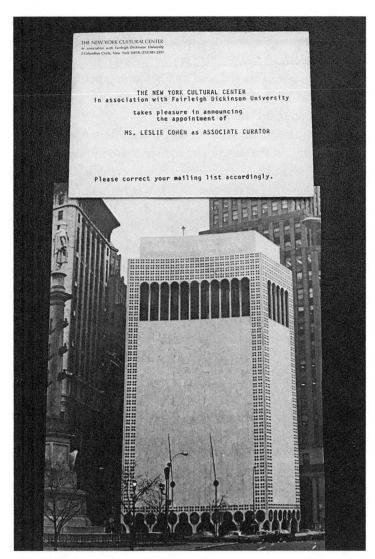

FIG. 13. The New York Cultural Center announcement, 1974.

and Doris Duke. I was invited to the gatherings of wealthy patrons and seated next to foreign consuls and rich benefactors. I met Larry Rivers, Salvador Dalí, Robert Rauschenberg, Jasper Johns, Roy Lichtenstein, Andy Warhol, and Robert Mapplethorpe, among others.

Being as young and inexperienced as I was, I often felt very insecure and tentative in this new role, like I did not belong in this
rarified world of art and wealth. I had barely left my mother's apartment. My sense of myself was finally forming but I still had a
long way to go. I felt overcome by the colossal glamour and
sophistication that I encountered.

On one particularly difficult day, Pincus-Witten was visiting
me in my office at the museum when I blurted out, "Robert, I don't
understand what I am doing here. I'm just a middle-class Jewish
girl from Queens." His response, delivered in his inimitable, unique
accent, was, "Leslie, *my dear*, don't you *know* that a middle-class
Jewish girl in *your* position is very *sexy*." What Robert was saying
was that mysteries were enticing to others. He had been incredibly adept at creating his own grand myth. Robert helped me understand how my background, in relation to the position I now held,
could be intriguing to others. It was a brilliant thing to say to me
and had a huge effect on how I viewed myself and acquired the
confidence I needed going forward.

The Museum was gaining notoriety and we did several consec-
utive high-visibility shows that were covered by all the leading
newspapers. I was proud of the exhibit *The American Nude* and the
high-profile Man Ray exhibition. We even had music by celebrated
composer Philip Glass, who played the Aeolian organ as background music at the opening of our Bal Blanc party. There were
massive crowds of people outside the museum, banging on the windows to get into the invitation-only party. I couldn't believe that
I was actually on the other side of the glass, no longer looking in.
I was in my dream job and mingling with the artistic, the rich,
and the famous. I was legit in every way except for one.

•

Once I had acknowledged to myself that I was gay, I became
immersed in the gay social world. The new lovers and friends that
I now had distanced me from my extremely close relationship with
my mother. In the past, we talked about everything, but our conversations had become stilted. Even though I loved her madly,
I had stopped sharing my private life with her. I did not talk to her

about my love affair with Suri or my present relationship with Michelle because I feared it would damage our bond. I was terrified to think that I might no longer be loved by my mother, that she might not want to have anything to do with me. It would be like losing the ground under my feet. Yet I longed for my mother's comfort and guidance, especially when my relationship with Suri ended and I was so heartbroken. I wanted to talk to her, for her to tell me everything would be all right. For a long while, there were no boyfriend stories to share, no mention of dates, no expression of any interest in men. We still spoke often but I evaded her questions about my love life.

•

My brother, Michael, and I had tried to form a relationship over the years as we became adults, but it was tough. Michael always struggled to get on his feet after he left the military. When he announced that he was driving to California to try and establish a new life for himself, I felt a strange nostalgia for that bond we had shared as children. I was happy that he had made a decision and hoped he would find his way, but I would miss him. I wanted to share something meaningful between us before he left, to help shorten the distance between us created by his past abuse. So much had happened to me that no one in my family knew about other than my cousin Ellen, and I didn't like hiding the truth about who I was. I figured, since my brother was moving to the other side of the country, I could tell him. It would remain our secret.

When I said the words, "I'm gay," he wasn't surprised.

"Oh, that's interesting. Makes sense considering where you come from," he said. It wasn't unexpected that he would make that assumption, considering the abuse we both experienced from my father.

"I really don't think it's because of Daddy, or you, for that matter. I really think I was born gay."

"Oh, okay," he said. He obviously did not want to debate the subject since I was in the process of revealing such an intimate part of myself to him.

"One last thing, though, Michael. Please don't tell Mommy. I don't want her to know. I don't know how she would handle it." He promised he wouldn't.

A few weeks later, I received a call from my mother telling me Michael was returning to New York. She said that he had gambled away his money in Las Vegas en route to California and had to come home. I felt bad for him; another one of his dreams had gone up in smoke.

After his return, he called me at my office. Usually, he never called me at work, so when I heard his voice, I worried that something had happened.

"Hi. Is anything wrong?"

"No, everything's fine except that I stopped in Vegas and went through all my money," he said.

"I know."

"I'm back on the couch until I can get my shit together."

"I know. You'll be okay."

Then he said, "By the way, I think Mommy knows you're gay."

I went numb. My voice started to shake. "What do you mean? How could she know? You're the only person I told!"

He could hear the panic in my voice and didn't know how to make it better. "Shit, Les, she's not stupid. She mentioned to me that you never talk about guys anymore, so I figured she knew."

"What?" I shouted.

Getting agitated, Michael said, "Mom's not an idiot you know. I think she just figured it out."

"And you confirmed it?" I shouted.

"What else could I do? I wasn't about to lie."

"Damn it! I told you not to tell her," I said, and hung up the phone, already freaking out.

I slumped back in my desk chair and stared out my office window overlooking Central Park. A state of anxiety overcame me that I couldn't shake off for the rest of the day. What did my mother think of me? Would she consider me a deviant? A misfit? A criminal? Would she be forever ashamed of me and shun me? The thought of losing her horrified me.

When I arrived home, I was a wreck. Just as I was telling Michelle what happened, the telephone rang. Michelle picked it up. I could see the apprehension on her face as she said, "Hi Marcia . . . yes, hold on, please." She handed me the telephone. "It's your mother."

Terrified, I took the phone from her hand and said, "Hi, Mama . . ."

Then, in her most comical, New York-ese, Yiddish affectation said, "*Soooo, I heard the good news!*" Her ironic humor and love, all combined in this one sentence, swept over me and I started to cry.

My mother said, "What's the matter, sweetheart?"

I responded in a breaking voice, "I thought you wouldn't love me anymore."

"I could never stop loving you. You are my daughter and I adore you."

And that was that. When I was able to speak, I said, "I'm sorry, Mama."

"There's nothing to be sorry about, darling. I want you to be happy; whatever makes you happy. That's all. Would I prefer you be with a man? Yes, of course; but only because I want security for you. I want your life to be easy. But I'm going to love you, no matter what."

Now my brother and mother knew and we were all still here. The world had changed again.

PART II

Freedom Calling

Choice is restorative when it reaches toward an
instinctive recognition of the earliest self.
—Frances Mayes, *Under the Tuscan Sun*[1]

7

Les Femmes

In 1974, "illegal, unethical, and improper" were the words that reporters used to describe the Watergate scandal that resulted in the historic resignation of Richard M. Nixon, the thirty-seventh president of the United States. It seemed like the country had fallen apart, not only morally but financially as well. A severe recession was also happening in the early 1970s because of OPEC's skyrocketing oil prices and its embargo of oil exports to the United States. Other factors contributing to the recession included heavy American government spending on the Vietnam War and a Wall Street stock market crash that hit in 1973 and continued in 1974.

One of the many victims of the recession was the New York Cultural Center. Shortly after I was hired in June 1974, Mario came into my office, closed the door, and tearfully told me that the museum was going to close in three months because of a lack of funds. Even the rich and philanthropic were hurting from their losses in the stock market and had severely cut back on donations to the museum. The wealthy family of Fairleigh Dickinson, who had made their fortune through the commercial production of the herbal remedy witch hazel and were the main benefactors of the museum, could no longer afford to support it.

"If you want to look for another job, I'll understand," Mario said.

It didn't take long for me to blurt out, "I'll stay." It was the only thing I could or wanted to do. Seeing Mario so distraught and frankly not knowing where else I could go, I knew that I had to try to save the museum for as long as possible. I had helped rescue *Artforum* during its financial crisis and I would do the same for the museum. I proceeded to take matters into my own hands, making heavy cuts in the budget and negotiating with the unions, which bought us more time. It was a constant struggle. I succeeded in keeping the museum open for another year and a half and helped mount some truly blockbuster exhibitions. Although my efforts were noble, they were not enough to save a sinking ship, and in October 1975, the museum finally closed.

•

During that stressful period, when I was totally preoccupied with work and sustaining the museum, I went dancing to relieve my anxiety, as I had so often done in the past. I went to lesbian bars all over Manhattan—the Lib, Bonnie and Clyde's, and the Tigress, among others—with Michelle and our best friends Barbara Russo and Linda Goldfarb. Dancing for hours on end was one of my favorite pastimes. But the more we went out, the more apparent it became that something was glaringly wrong with the scene. None of the clubs were actually owned by women, which explained the schlocky, run-down nature of most of these Mafia-owned haunts. From the dance floor, I often looked around at the dingy surroundings, the worn and bland décor, and asked myself why we continued to patronize these clubs. They lacked any semblance of style and class. How were women supposed to feel self-respect and dignity in these environments?

Don't get me wrong; I had a ball anyway. I danced my ass off, young and sexed up, but my friends and I wondered why there weren't any women opening their own bars or nightclubs—something edgy, contemporary, sophisticated—something that we would be proud to be seen in, that would be hip enough for how cool we were; instead, we were forced to slum at these dives because that's all there was.

The gay nightclubs for women that existed in the 1970s were still stuck in the mentality of the repressive 1950s. Although there *were* elegant gay men's clubs, it was obvious that the men who owned and ran the lesbian clubs still regarded women as inferior, second-class citizens and lesbians as society's outcasts. And, sadly, women could not do anything to change the situation because of the oppressive dictates set by a male-dominated, homophobic society. Lesbians were forced to stay closeted or risk losing their jobs or worse, their *children*. Women had little or no access to credit, which made it very difficult to open a business. As often as we heard other women ask why there wasn't a refined nightclub run by women for themselves, no one seemed to have the answer. The truth was that no one had the resources, knowledge, or gumption to dare and do it.

That's when Michelle and I started to toy with the idea of opening a club. Why not us? We were attractive, young, hip, well-educated, post-Stonewall lesbians with the audacity to consider creating a club of our own. Times were trying to change. And once Michelle set her mind to something, she was determined to make it happen. She was the engine that made our dream possible. Barbara and Linda, our friends, with whom we had shared everything in the past, would soon join us in the endeavor.

•

Barbara Russo was a close friend of mine from Queens College when I was a graduate student and she was an undergraduate hanging out in the faculty cafeteria. She was gregarious, affectionate, generous, and attractive. Later, after we left Queens College, and not knowing that I was a lesbian and in a relationship with Michelle (which might have helped her accept who she was), she tried the proverbial marriage of convenience with a gay guy. She didn't know or admit she was a lesbian until *after* her marriage failed. She still jokes that I almost ruined her life by not telling her about myself sooner.

When Michelle and I introduced her to Linda Goldfarb, a close high school friend of Michelle's from Long Island, they became a couple. Linda had a wicked sense of humor like Michelle's and a dry wit. She had a quiet, sultry sexiness about her. The four of us spent a lot of time together, so when Michelle and I told Linda and Barbara of our plan to open a nightclub for women, they immediately wanted in. Linda sealed the deal by saying her father would back us financially. We thought we were off to a good start.

The mere idea of owning a nightclub was very risky and extremely exhilarating at the same time. Every day expanded our vision for the club. As farfetched as it seemed, the more we talked about it, the more real it became in our minds.

Our hope was that our club would be the exact opposite of all those that existed. It would be elegant, stylish, and a true cultural center for women. My passion for the idea was fueled by my deep love of women and my love of art. I truly believed that lesbians were the coolest people in the world. I was inspired by the early twentieth-century lesbians I deeply admired, like Natalie Barney, Virginia Woolf, Colette, Romaine Brooks, Gertrude Stein, and Alice B. Toklas, who were just a few of the fascinating women who paved the way for lesbian high culture. Because of their art, books, poetry, and outspoken lifestyles, they were the women I wanted to emulate.

It was salon culture, where artists came to share and discuss their work in intimate gatherings, that intrigued me and that I wanted to replicate. These gatherings took place in private homes in Paris and London. I wanted a nightclub with a salon feel, a place that encouraged an exchange of ideas, a place that introduced the world to the creativity and ingenuity of women. From where I stood, lesbians were bold and creative in every aspect of their lives. It was not only their work that I celebrated; it was their fearless thinking that inspired me to accomplish what we were attempting to do. By adding a cultural and political edge to the club, we would have a concept that had never existed before. With the advent of the gay rights and women's liberation movements, the time was ripe. As a curator and feminist, it was a natural progression for me.

The process of creating the nightclub turned out to be the most significant learning curve of my life. It didn't take long for me to see that owning and running a club was a massive, all-consuming enterprise. Naively, I thought that I could just be the visionary behind the scenes, and the club would magically appear and operate on its own. I thought I would go back to the art world. I never imagined how deeply involved I would get.

The time spent dreaming and designing the club until the day we opened our doors was a whirlwind. Barbara (whom I had gotten a job at the museum as Mario's assistant) and I hung on at the museum, but when it closed, to make ends meet, I worked with Linda at her father's insurance company. Barbara got a job as a bartender at La Femme, another Mafia-owned lesbian bar that we frequented in the West Village. She took the job to learn how to set up a bar and to absorb everything she could about the business. Michelle was working at an advertising production company representing film directors, shopping their reels and trying to get them commercial work. Stuck in the job for strictly financial reasons, she was also unsatisfied. No matter what else we were doing to pay our bills, our minds were now always on the club.

•

Ignorance is bliss, as they say. Back in 1975, we were *so* naive, unaware of the laws in place to discriminate against gays and lesbians and the resulting deep Mafia involvement in gay clubs. Outrageous laws made it illegal to even *attempt* to open a gay bar. If we had known the half of it, we probably wouldn't have tried. I was aware of the burgeoning gay rights movement and had volunteered at the nascent National Gay Task Force in late 1974 (before they added "Lesbian" to the title). The oppression and stigma against gays and lesbians and the darkness and fear surrounding our lives made no sense to me. As far as I was concerned, we had no reason to be ashamed of our love. We were *loved*—as someone's child, friend, aunt, uncle, employee, or employer—before. Why should my sexual preference now make me a pariah? What was the *fucking* big deal? That was our attitude as we set up the club. The four of us were determined to challenge the deeply ingrained status quo.

Thanks to Linda's father, we thought our financing was in place, so Michelle quit her job to start the search for a suitable space for the club. Michelle and I struggled with only my income to rely on, which put a heavy strain on our relationship. Frugality was something she had never practiced, but I had been living that way my whole life.

Besides the money stress, Michelle was fed up with my dalliances with outside lovers. She always knew what I was up to because when she confronted me, I broke out in hives. For example, I had to confess to her my encounter with a Latin journalist that I met on the subway on my way to City College where I was taking a course. After we had had a pleasant lunch together, I brought him home for sex. But to my chagrin, instead of the lovemaking I was expecting, he sat me down on the edge of the bed, stood before me, opened his fly, and pulled my head to him. After he was done, there was no attempt on his part to satisfy me. I said nothing. It was clear that I still did not have the fortitude to assert myself with men and either stop him and demand what I wanted or insist that he satisfy me, too. I was deeply disappointed in myself.

When Michelle came home and found I had made the bed, which was something I rarely did, she looked at me suspiciously and questioned me. As usual, I broke out in hives and confessed. I tried to assure her that this escapade didn't mean anything and that I was just trying to gauge my place on the sexual spectrum, but it was too late.

I deserved what I got. Michelle started an affair with a woman named Judith. Judith adored her. It was more than a mere dalliance for Michelle, but she was still taken by surprise and shocked when I packed her suitcase one day and left it in the hallway. I ended our relationship, and Michelle moved in with Judith. Soon after, I moved into a walkup on East 73rd Street by myself.

Michelle and I were together for over three years. I sorely missed her companionship and our deep friendship. On the other hand, I looked forward to living on my own. My belief in everlasting love had eroded after Suri anyway and my dissolved relationship with Michelle just confirmed it. I decided I would never find "the love of my life" and chalked the whole romantic ideal up to a childish fantasy perpetrated by books and the media. I figured I would be fine with serial love affairs. And despite our breakup, Michelle would never be too far away anyway; we still had a club to open.

•

Meanwhile, Linda's father, Seymour, backpedaled on his promise to invest in our club. Instead, he introduced us to two of his friends, Joe and Tommy, who were interested in investing. Joe and Tommy were Italian guys who grew up on the tough streets of Brooklyn. According to Seymour, they had both done well in the insurance business. And to ease any discomfort, Seymour assured us that they were *not* connected to the Mafia.

The guys were the stereotypical 1970s "swinger" types who parked their wives and children in the suburbs of New Jersey while they gallivanted around the city. Joe was tall and skinny like an elongated tree trunk. He wore immaculately pressed polyester suits. His voice was quiet and spare. Despite his appearance, he had a stable, businesslike quality about him. Tommy, on the other hand, was short and good-looking. He was well built and had a belligerent, bombastic way about him. He walked with a strut, wore skin-tight pants and fishnet shirts, and layered his neck with gold chains. Whenever Tommy was around women, he felt compelled to make a sexual impression.

We held our "business meetings" in their apartment, located on a seedy part of Eighth Avenue in the West 50s, known for its sex workers, pimps, and endless rows of pornographic movie theaters. Their "bachelor pad" was cheaply decorated with a brown, faux leather couch, orange shag rug, a glass-and-chrome coffee table, and two matching side tables. Prostitutes occupied most of the apartments in the building, rented by their pimps so the women had a place to go to get off the streets and turn tricks. Joe and Tommy's apartment served the same purpose. For them, it was their go-to place to get laid.

In our meetings there, we all sat around drinking coffee from Styrofoam cups, which cluttered the room along with ashtrays filled with cigarette butts. Whenever Tommy or Joe needed a break from our shoptalk, they made us watch their homemade porn films featuring their sex worker friends, as if they were showing us their bowling trophies. While the porn films played, Barbara, Michelle, Linda, and I surreptitiously exchanged dismayed glances as we laughed along with Joe and Tommy, trying to pretend that we were just one of the guys.

Often offended by their brusque and sexist behavior, we had to sweep our reactions under the shag rug to placate them because they had the money and we had no one else to turn to. Ironically, here we were, doing what women always did to please men and get their way: playing along, downplaying our own needs, laughing, and kissing ass so that we could get the money we needed. While I was trying to sell them on my feminist and art-infused ideas about an elegant club for women that was so au courant that the art and literary worlds would feel compelled to be there, I wished I could put a towel down before I sat on their couch. My words and ideas just sailed over their heads. The tension of appeasement was always there. We rationalized: "They aren't bad guys." "We'll make it happen." "What choice do we have?" That's how badly we wanted to open this club. We called them Tweedledee and Tweedledum. The only good thing about this series of meetings was that, finally, Tweedledee and Tweedledum seemed to be on board and agreed to back us.

•

Michelle found a space on Broadway and 4th Street that we nicknamed the Colosseum because it was so gigantic. It was an empty, unfinished shell with debris lying all around. Overly enthusiastic in her usual way, Michelle wanted us to go see it with Joe and Tommy and their contractor. When we arrived, we followed the three men around the large area like unwanted appendages, trying to hear what they were saying. We watched them pointing, shaking their heads, and gesturing with their hands, ignoring us. Once in a while, numbers and unfamiliar plumbing, wiring, and heating terms were discernable through the distance between us.

Finally, the contractor, a large, beefy man with a red face, looked directly at Tommy and Joe and said, "I don't want to discourage you, but I don't think you could put this place together for less than $100,000." Then he looked over at us as an afterthought and said,

"Oh yeah, and you gotta put in whatever money the girls need for decorations."

Facetiously, Michelle said under her breath, "Yeah, crepe paper and colored balloons!"

When we went back to their apartment to further discuss the prospect, Tommy turned to Michelle and said, "It may be the size of the fucking Colosseum, but you better be sure as shit that Joe and I are not the fucking Roman Empire!"

"Take it easy, Tommy," Joe said, "we're all disappointed."

Trying to deflect the hostility, Linda, who was looking out the window, said, "Couldn't you guys find a nicer neighborhood to trick in?"

Tommy laughed. "Listen to Seymour's daughter. You're too much! My 'girls' live and work here. Why should I make them travel?"

The "girls" he was referring to were the prostitutes.

He turned to Joe. "She's all right. Now if she only has Seymour's business head, we'll make a lot of money."

Bored of the shoptalk, Tommy added, "Look, if you girls would excuse me, I'd like to get laid now," and stood up from the couch, ending the conversation.

Michelle asked, "Tommy, you guys really only sleep with hookers? That must be nice for your wives."

Tommy answered with an evil grin. "Yeah. The good news is that we don't pay."

I contributed, "You're *that* good?"

"It's not me," answered Tommy. "I have no control. It's Joe that they love. He stays hard for so long he forgets he's fucking!" Using his thumb to point to Joe, he continued his tribute. "This guy eats dinner, watches television, and calls his wife while he's fucking! It's an amazing thing to watch!"

We laughed appeasingly once again. I couldn't help but wonder, what the hell were we doing there?

•

The next space Michelle found was on the Upper East Side, on East 65th Street and Second Avenue. The address was 1234

Second Avenue. It was a small two-story building that had formerly been an Indian restaurant. A kitchen fire had damaged the restaurant's interior. The restaurant owner, Harris, was asking $30,000 for us to take over the lease. When we told Joe and Tommy about it, they told us to arrange a meeting, which really raised our hopes that this club was going to happen.

However, right before the meeting with Harris, Tweedledee and Tweedledum sprang the unexpected on us. "We need you girls to contribute fifty percent. You girls must have $15,000, don't cha?" All along, it was clear to everyone that their role was as financial backers and we were to be the operating partners. The whole point of our partnership was we needed them for their money, obviously not their expertise. Now that we were getting closer to making it a reality, they were copping out. There was no point in trying to work it out with them. They were steadfast. Our "partnership" with Tweedledee and Tweedledum fell apart on the spot.

So here we were, four young women in 1975 on the brink of a meeting with Harris, the owner of the Indian restaurant, with absolutely no financial backing. I wasn't upset about losing the guys because they really had no clue about what we were trying to do. But we had already wasted so much time waiting for Linda's dad, and even more time with Tweedledee and Tweedledum, and now we were back to square one. "Why are we even going to this meeting?" I asked. But Michelle insisted. That afternoon, we kept the appointment with Harris. As we approached the storefront, we could only hope for a miracle. We had no money. How was this club ever going to happen? It seemed hopeless.

The restaurant's damaged interior was dingy, dark, and reeked from the smell of smoke that had seeped up from the kitchen fire in the basement below. In a brilliant move, Michelle pulled the proverbial rabbit out of the hat. As we walked into the building and saw Harris standing in the front, Michelle confidently said, "Thanks for meeting with us, Harris. We actually have a better deal for you than what we talked about before."

His eyes widened. "What is that?"

Barbara, Linda, and I looked at each other stupefied, not having any idea what Michelle was talking about.

"Let's forgo the $30,000 buyout we discussed and instead offer you fifty percent of our business."

The three of us stood there in awe and disbelief. We couldn't believe that Michelle had come up with that off the top of her head. Like I said, Michelle makes things happen. We all held our breath, awaiting his answer.

Harris stood silent, thinking about it.

Finally, he said, "Okay, I accept . . . but I'll still need $4,000 to renew the lease and pay the security deposit."

Michelle said, "Fine, that works," with no idea where we were going to get $4,000.

As I stood there, bewildered, wondering how we were going to find the money, she said to Harris, "We'll meet you at the bank (the restaurant was a bank-owned property) with the money when you're scheduled to sign the lease."

We left the meeting giddy and incredulous about what just happened. Harris went for it! We almost had a space, but no backing, and not one red cent to our names. Harris had absolutely zero to lose except a burnt-out restaurant with no business, and we also had absolutely nothing to lose because, well, we had nothing, nada, zilch! We were all drowning and offering each other life preservers made of cotton.

"I need a drink," Linda said. One drink turned into many over the next few days. We worked closely with Sid Davidoff, the lawyer referred to us by Seymour Goldfarb. Davidoff was a die-hard progressive. It was obvious that he was smart and a champion for the underdog, which is what we had turned into overnight.

Sid couldn't believe that four naive young women were actually trying to open a club for women in New York City in 1975. Up until 1974, women still needed their husbands or, for single women, a male relative to cosign applications for a credit card or to open a bank account. We had all been so removed from the business world that we weren't really aware of those limitations. We even met with the newly opened Women's Bank to try to get a loan, but since we had no assets, they refused our request. We were stronger together, or perhaps just plain delusional about the realities of opening a club, but we just kept pushing on.

After mulling the case over, Sid decided he was interested in working with us. When he asked Michelle how we planned on paying for his services, we all went silent. Even Michelle took a minute to answer. We all looked down at our shoes until Michelle looked over at Barbara and jokingly said, "Barb will give you head!" Sid could not believe his ears. It became the standing joke and whenever Sid asked for his money, we would all simultaneously turn to Barbara and say, "Barb, give him head!"

Impressed with our gumption, Sid agreed to wait for his money. Looking at all angles of our situation, he quickly advised us to take a different approach to setting up the business. "You don't need to give Harris fifty percent," he said. "He's not contributing anything to the partnership. Think about it. He has no money; his lease is up; he has no functioning business; and the place is fire damaged. Let me call the bank and request the right of first refusal if Harris doesn't show up at the lease signing."

It made total sense to everyone but Michelle, who was hesitant because she gave her word to Harris. At that point, however, whatever Sid advised, we agreed to do. Linda talked to her father, who agreed to give us $4,000 for the deposit.

Sid waited outside the landlord's office at the bank on the day of the lease signing. Michelle stayed in bed with a blanket over her head, avoiding Harris's phone calls to confirm the meeting. As the minutes turned into hours, we anxiously awaited our fate.

By nightfall on December 8, 1975, as Sid predicted, Harris didn't show up to sign the lease. We were able to exercise our right of first refusal, and signed a ten-year lease for the property. Our tenure would begin February 15, 1976. We were elated, but then the reality set in. We had the $4,000 deposit from Linda's father, but no other money to build out and supply a nightclub. What were we thinking? I was in a daze. Suddenly, I would have to find money I didn't have. The country was nearing the end of an economic recession, the most severe since World War II. This clearly was not the ideal time to borrow money or find investors for a lesbian bar.

•

The only stable thing around us was that Barbara was still busy bartending at La Femme. One night, Linda, Michelle, and I went to La Femme, located a block off Washington Square, to see her. As usual, a large male bouncer, whose eyes scanned us up and down as though he was performing an MRI, greeted us at the door. Once we stepped inside, there were two more beefy men lingering at the bar. This was clearly a club run by men. We made a mental note; our club would *not* be like that.

We saw Barbara behind the bar, shaking drinks above her head with her usual gregarious smile. We sat on barstools, watching her skillfully smack the side of the mixing cup with her hand to free the glass and then pour the drink from high above, watching it fall toward the glass like a waterfall. She was showing off for us and we knew it. We were proud of her.

She leaned over the bar and whispered, "You don't have to worry about a thing. I know how to set up a bar now. I've even made drawings."

"Really?" I asked, relieved, because none of us had ever worked in a bar before, let alone owned one.

"You see, they have different keys on the register for booze, juice, and beer—that's how they keep control of the inventory. Then the bartenders and waitresses have different keys so the owners know how much money each of us is putting into the register."

As Barbara shared her knowledge, a customer waved her down to get a drink. Barbara held up her pointer finger to wait.

Linda and I both struggled to understand the bar system that Barbara had just explained. Shaking our heads in unison, we said, "We don't get it."

Michelle said, "Okay, got it. What else?"

"I'll explain it all later," Barbara said as she fielded heckling from the impatient customer who yelled down the bar, "How does some-one get a drink around here?"

Linda looked over at the woman, smiled sweetly, and then turned back to Barbara, whispering, "Watch out she doesn't bite your hand off! She looks like a Chihuahua."

Barbara pulled Linda toward her over the bar, kissed her, and then pointing to our drinks, said, "You okay? It's on the house."

Watching the busy action at the bar, I realized that this scenario would soon be ours. I said to Barbara, "Go serve your customers before you get fired. Besides, we need the money!"

•

The four of us spent every spare moment thinking about the bar. We had figured out that we needed about $36,000 to open the doors with a bare-bones build-out. We needed money for utility deposits, construction, sound, lights, salaries, carpeting, furniture, painting, glasses, registers, insurance, an awning, grand opening invitations, advertisements, and booze. Once we opened the doors and started to earn income, we planned to do more.

Sid managed to procure a $6,000 loan from the company that would install our vending machines. We would pay them back with the proceeds from the jukebox, cigarette machine, and pinball machine. Just $30,000 more to go. Despite our lack of funds, we began interviewing contractors and sound and lighting people. Sid worked on getting our liquor license and a zoning variance for our cabaret license, which allowed dancing. Both licenses would take months to procure.

Without any backers, we had to go to the banks ourselves. But without any credit history of our own, we all needed cosigners, someone with a strong financial history who could guarantee the loans for us. Seymour agreed to cosign the loans for Barbara and Linda, so that was the first $12,000. Judith, Michelle's new lover, owned a house, and had the credit to cosign a loan for Michelle for $6,000. With her additional assets, Judith put in another $6,000, thus becoming a silent partner. There was now $30,000 in the pot. I was the only one without any money. I needed $6,000 and had zero dollars and nowhere to turn. No one in my family had any assets to secure and cosign a loan for me—not my mother, my brother Michael, my aunts, uncles, or cousins. Since my deceased father left no will, his new wife had inherited all of his assets. Michael and I ended up with nothing.

I was so desperate that I asked Robert Pincus-Witten, but he said no. I even asked John, my graduate school friend, and he also said no. They were both kind in their refusals, but I understood that there was no way they would risk their own credit to cosign a loan for me to open a lesbian bar in 1976. It was as far-fetched as it sounded. Asking for help was excruciating because I had never asked anyone for anything before except from my father, and that was emotional torture. My mother agreed to lend me her total savings of $1,000.

Obviously, the $1,000 was not enough, and the reality, which was becoming more and more real by the day, was that I would have to leave the partnership, which was crushing. I had already put so much of my heart and soul into planning the club. One night, anxious and depressed, I went out to dinner with Carolee, a friend I had started dating. I wanted to take my mind off of my problems.

The first thing she said to me when I sat down at the table was, "What happened to you? You look terrible."

I said, "I don't have my portion of the money I need for the club. I've asked my family. They don't have any money. My mother feels terrible and lent me all that she has, which was her entire savings of $1,000. Out of the $6,000 I need to raise, I'm still short $5,000. I need a loan, but I don't have a cosigner to guarantee it. There's nothing else I can do."

Without any hesitation, squeezing my hand, Carolee said, "I'll cosign the loan for you."

I would have never thought to ask Carolee even though she had the resources. It would have been inappropriate. We had been acquaintances before, but we had just started dating. Any rational person would have told her not to lend me money for a nightclub. I even felt awkward accepting it, but I knew that there was no way in hell that I wouldn't repay her. I'd sweep floors if I had to. I knew that, but how could she? Carolee was willing to take an enormous chance on me, and I remain eternally grateful. Because of her I was in. The club was a go.

8

Water in the Desert

The city and state authorities that we relied on for our licensing put us through the wringer. Of course, we did not tell them that we planned to open a gay club because that would have stymied any chance of our succeeding. It was hard enough being women. On top of that, we were young. We were still in our twenties. The authorities just did not take us seriously. Barbara, Linda, Michelle, and I might have been the first women in years to apply for a state liquor license and cabaret license in New York City. The guy from the State Liquor Authority (SLA) actually had the gall to say, "I have your application in front of me, but in order to move this thing forward, we'll need an affidavit from your nearest *male* relative." It turns out they thought we were possibly a front for the Mafia or prostitutes, when our only crime was being young and female. I don't doubt for a minute that if they had known we were gay they would have found some excuse to deny us a liquor license. Some things you keep to yourself; other things you just can't hide.

"Really?" Barbara said to the man at the SLA. "I don't have one. I don't have any male siblings and my father's dead. So, now what?"

Getting a liquor license became the one battle that we left for our lawyer. A liquor license for a group of women raised questions because it was so rare. Sid Davidoff wanted to score a historic notch on his belt, which is why he took on our impossible, nonlucrative case in the first place, so we let him smooth the way with the state authorities to take the focus off the fact that we were women.

Besides, we had more important things to do, like come up with a name for the club. Finally, we agreed on the name Mirage. Michelle and I had consulted with a psychic medium in the past, so we thought we would run the name by her. She was our only attempt at a focus group or any real market research. Her name was Reverend Woodbury and she lived in that iconic rococo behemoth, the Ansonia Hotel, on Broadway on the Upper West Side, which has been home to such illustrious characters as Babe Ruth, Igor Stravinsky, and Natalie Portman. But, after we came back from seeing her, our hopes of using the name Mirage were dashed.

Linda and Barbara had been on pins and needles waiting for the psychic's approval. I broke the news: "We can't use the name Mirage."

"Why the hell not?" Linda said.

Michelle said, "The psychic broke the word down phonetically. When you break the name into syllables, it is 'my' and 'rage.'"

They both gasped, "Oh no!"

Linda said, "We have invested every penny we have in this club . . ."

Barbara jumped in, "The last thing we need is a name that is a bummer."

Time was running out. We really needed a name so that the canopy leading into the club could be delivered in time for the opening. The next day, Barbara walked into the construction mess that would soon be the club. She happened to be wearing a T-shirt with a picture of a caravan of nomads crossing the desert. In French, it read: "Retour au Sahara." Looking down at her chest, Barbara's eyes suddenly widened. "I think I've found the name," she said. "What do you think of the name 'Sahara'?"

We all went silent. Michelle finally said, "According to Reverend Woodbury, *H* is a money letter, so Sahara fulfills the requirement. Yes, Sahara is the name!"

"Yes!" I echoed. I loved it. Our club would be an oasis in the desert of conformity. It would be a place in the world where women could feel self-respected and safe. For my whole life I had heard society saying to women, *no, you're not worth it*.

Sahara was going to say, *yes, we are!*

•

I knew that Sid would make it happen. I knew he would be able to get us our liquor license, and once he did, I also knew that my life would never be the same. As Barbara said, "The closet was a very big place and it housed most of us." When the doors of Sahara eventually opened, I'd be "out" in a big way.

The courage that I mustered to open the club didn't come overnight. It was a gradual process that was not fueled by individual chutzpah alone. More decisively, Sahara would never have materialized without the mutual fortitude, love and support of all of us—me, Michelle, Barbara, and Linda. But, as the doors to Sahara were about to open, little did I know that more than my thirst for equality and respect for women and lesbians would be quenched.

•

In April of 1976, a few weeks before Sahara was to open, my college friend Dotty called me from her showroom in the garment district. When I picked up, she shouted excitedly into the phone, "You are *not* going to believe who's here with me!"

"Who?" I asked.

Dotty replied, "Beth Suskin!"

I felt a tingle pass through me as if a tiny fish had traversed my veins. "What?" I exclaimed. "Wow! I don't believe it. She's there now?"

"Yes. She came in for a job interview and I just hired her! Hold on," Dotty said and she passed the phone to Beth.

Beth said, "Leslie, can you believe this? What a crazy coincidence!"

Once I caught my breath, I responded, "No, I can't believe it! This is insane."

There were superlatives, exclamations, and brief explanations all mashed into two or three minutes. Finally, I suggested a get-together at my apartment with some of our other college friends.

I had not spoken to Beth Suskin since she transferred from Buffalo State to Hofstra University on Long Island to be near her boyfriend Sean ten years before. I felt an exhilaration that left me flushed. Later that night, I called Dotty to hear more details about Beth's reappearance in our lives. Dotty said, "I put an ad in the paper. I was looking for someone to help in the showroom."

"What an insane coincidence," I said.

"Yes, it is." After a pause, Dotty said, "Leslie, she asked if you are with anyone and I told her you're gay."

I said, "Really? What did she say?"

"She said she wasn't surprised."

"Interesting."

"Yes. She said she always felt there was something different about you."

•

It was Saturday night and the small living room in my fourth-floor walk-up apartment on East 73rd Street was crammed with Dot, Adrienne, Ellen (another college friend), and Beth. The room had wall-to-wall pink carpeting, a lime-green velvet club chair, a rust-colored corduroy couch, and floor-to-ceiling bookshelves, all furniture that I had brought over from my other apartment with Michelle, which mixed with the leftovers from the previous tenant. I laid out some cheese and crackers and a couple of bottles of wine for my guests on the small round marble table that doubled as my desk and dining table. Hanging between the two leaded windows facing the street was my cherished signed Giorgio de Chirico lithograph, a gift from Mario Amaya. In the background, I could hear the sound of children playing on the street below and the hiss of the radiator in the room.

As Beth sat in front of me again for the first time in ten years, I studied her—natural, long, wavy brown hair (that I had remembered in college as shorter, straight, and blonde), little makeup, and a peasant blouse and jeans. Her look had become more bohemian then French in style, but she was still incredibly beautiful. My senses were fully piqued by her presence.

Effortlessly, with that familiar pull we had felt in the past, Beth and I talked as though we had just been waiting to hear each other's voices again. We became so totally engrossed in each other's company as we began to fill each other in on our lives, that our other friends were relegated to mere extras in the scene, like blurred shadows in the background.

The deep connection that we felt in college had been buried but never left us. No matter what had transpired over the last ten years of our lives, there was always a piece of me that wondered about Beth, what she was doing, and how she had managed the difficult parts of her life that she had shared with me.

"Catch me up," I said.

"As you know, I transferred in the fall of 1967 to Hofstra University on Long Island." Her voice lowered. "I was lonely for Sean and wanted to be near him."

As she told her story, I heard the key words: obsessive, jealousy, and controlling nature.

I already knew that but still found it hard to believe that, in spite of his emotional abuse, she had remained with him as long as she did. Obsessed with him since the age of twelve, she mistook his pathological jealousy, his need to control everything in her life, for love.

Then she said, "I believed he would change once I married him. But instead, my life became a living hell . . ." After a moment, she continued. "When I was nineteen, as a favor to my parents, I started to sing on demos for two songwriters they knew who were trying to sell their songs. You remember I used to sing in high school?"

"Yes," I said, nodding.

"Two guys from Buddah Records heard me on the demo and offered me a recording contract and . . ."

"Really? Wow, that's a major record company," I interrupted. "That must have been fantastic! You had such a beautiful voice."

The other girls chimed in in agreement. They were all familiar with her terrific reputation in high school as the lead singer for the Valiants on Long Island. Beth's eyes glazed over. Perhaps she was also thinking about those nights we shared jamming in the tunnel. She looked up as though she had awoken from a dream and continued. "But Sean made me give it up. He didn't want me to do it. He was afraid that other men would see me onstage and take me from him. He was so paranoid he wouldn't even let me see the Beatles at Shea Stadium." She smiled a sad smile.

Adrienne cursed him. "What an asshole! How did you stay with him?"

"He sounds pathological," I said.

Angered, I reached for another glass of wine as she laid out more of the facts. Sean withheld sex from her as soon as they got married as a test of her devotion to him. As his paranoia increased and his possessiveness and abuse intensified, she shut down and withdrew from the world. She spent the majority of the next six years predominately in bed, alone—agoraphobic, isolated, and deeply depressed. Her only companion was her dog, Damian. We all listened intently as she continued, but it was on me that Beth's eyes remained locked.

Her wine glass had emptied and I got up to pour her some more. "One night, during an argument," she said, her voice low and steady, "he threw me to the floor, pinned me down, shook his finger violently in my face and shouted, 'SHUT UP!'"

With her wine glass in hand, she paused. "I hope I'm not talking too much," she said.

"No, not at all. Go on," we all said in unison.

"I knew I was in physical danger, and I was terrified, but at that moment something finally clicked in me and I knew the marriage was over."

"Amen!" Dotty shouted.

I asked, "What did you do then?

Beth said, "The next day while he was at work, I packed a suitcase with whatever I could fit inside and went to my parents. This time, no matter how much he pleaded with me to come back, that he was sorry and would change, which I had heard a million times before, I had finally had enough."

"What did you do after that?"

"I stayed with my parents and then, a few months after my divorce, I met Steven on a blind date, and that's who I'm with now."

"Another guy so soon?" Ellen said, alarmed.

She paused to see if anyone else would have the same reaction. When it was silent, she continued. "We fell for each other immediately. We slept together and I never left. I know I can be very impulsive, but it's what I wanted. I knew right away that it was right. He's not *at all* like Sean. He's very sweet and affectionate." Her eyes softened. "He's very sexy. He looks like Mick Jagger. We've been together for three years now."

She looked around the room to emphasize that.

"Well, that's good. At least you're happy and you met someone who is good to you," I said.

"He's very open. He's a nice guy. He loves me deeply, which helped so much with my healing, but . . ." She paused trying to find the right words.

I sensed a void. Something was missing. Then she said these pivotal words: "Sometimes, I feel like I need more than he can give me. As wonderful as he is . . ."

"What do you mean?" I asked.

Almost apologetically, she said, "I wish he had more psychological insight, and that he was more artistic, creative. I need more intellectual stimulation. But that's just not who he is."

I understood her frustration. I didn't want to push her any further, and frankly felt sad that she was with someone who left her wanting more. More importantly, I could hear in the prosaic description of her relationship with Steven that she was falling out of love with him. To change the subject, she turned to me and said, "Enough about me. Tell me about you, Les."

So much had happened in the last ten years that I didn't know where to begin. I gave her the bullet points. "Well, I went to graduate school after college and got a master's degree in art history. I had a pretty impressive career in the art world. I worked for *Artforum* magazine and became a curator of a well-known museum. But now I'm about to open a nightclub for women. Crazy, huh? You know I'm gay, right?"

"Yes, I know," she said, this time to my face. "You always had this androgynous way about you," she said, looking at me affectionately.

I smiled at her. "I'm opening this club for women with some friends because what's been out there for so long is dreck and our club is going to be very special. We open in three weeks. The experience is both exciting and scary because I have everything riding on this."

"That's incredible. You're very bold. It sounds great . . . are you still wild like you were in college?"

Adrienne kicked in, "She's worse than ever!"

We laughed. "I guess I am because I'm about to take the wildest ride of my life by opening this club. I hope you'll come to the opening with the girls . . ."

"I'd love to come." Beth looked at me closely for a moment and then said, "Do you mind if I ask you a personal question?"

"Of course not," I responded.

"What is it about women that you like?"

It was unusual for someone to be so blatantly curious about my sexuality and I admired her for that. All the girls turned to me to see my response. My answer was immediate. Looking directly at Beth, I said, "Their skin—the softness of their skin."

In the background, Ellen chimed in, "You never told *us* that."

"You never asked!" I said, and everyone laughed.

Beth began asking me pointed questions. How and when did I know I was gay? What was gay life like? Did I miss men? Beth's interest intrigued me. I did not find her questions inappropriate at all and welcomed her openness about a subject that others felt was too taboo to broach. Once again, the circle closed in around us as we were pulled back into that electrically charged bubble that we had generated together a decade ago. Although the small room was full of my old college friends and their laughter, as far as I was concerned, she was the only person there.

I was captivated by her innocence, her enthusiasm, her inquisitiveness. I watched her full lips move as they surrounded her words, listening to the very specific up-and-down cadence of her voice and her strange laughter that broke out into a loud cackle when something struck her as very funny—it would shock you upon hearing it because it was so incongruous to her femininity and beauty. She still had that totally unique and imaginative way of talking with metaphors that distinguished her in college. I was falling in love with each gesture and utterance she made. Although she had let herself be abused by Sean, she still seemed wild and untamable like the girl I had met that first day in college. She was contradictory in so many ways—fearful yet bold, soft yet tough, mad as a hatter yet grounded, insanely funny yet fraught with self-doubt and shame. I so wanted to pull her to me, to embrace her and feel her soft cheek pressed against mine.

I knew I loved her right then and that I could be with her forever. You might ask, *Forever? All of this came from this first meeting after so many years?* The only answer is yes. It was like a lifetime compressed in the flash of a moment. The connection we had that night was so deep and soulful, so loving, that my intuition about it was based on something that was beyond this earth and utterly mysterious; yet I did not doubt it.

After everyone left with promises to see me at the opening of the club, I washed the dishes and cleaned up the apartment, but Beth lingered. For someone who had given up on any notion of finding, or even believing in, forever love, the thought that she could be that for me was quite remarkable. But I also knew there was nothing I could do about it. She was straight, so I would never expect or hope for anything more than a renewed friendship with an old college friend as it would have been foolish for me to do so. Yet I still knew how I felt about her.

9

Jagged, Dirty Thoughts

What induced me to want to open a nightclub for women and risk everything that I had worked for and attained in my art career? I thought about this a lot. I would be outing myself in a grand way and knew I would be forever after labeled as a "lesbian," a label that would box me in and obscure all the other facets of who I was in the eyes of the world. This would create a huge barrier to any future career in the art world that I might fathom, even in the supposedly sophisticated and urbane art world of New York City in 1976 (which, in reality, was as homophobic and patriarchal as any other subculture at that time). Building up the self-confidence to risk ostracism in order to follow my own inclinations did not just magically happen. It was a gradual process of changing my outlook, though it was certainly the result of a buildup of frustration from the many limitations and constraints imposed on women by society. Fighting that battle was as important to me as changing society's archaic attitudes about sexual orientation.

I was driven in those days, determined to make my point, which was that women could not be shoved into a box and demeaned no matter how hard the world tried. On the many nights I ruminated on my desire for change, I'd retreat to my diary to express my frustrations about being a woman in a man's world:

I want to write a script of my life that's intriguing. I want to be James Dean in drag. Damn it! Men are not the only ones with lives. Women have lives too. Women are James Dean too. Just look at the movies. They feature Jack Nicholson in *One Flew over the Cuckoo's Nest*, Al Pacino in *Dog Day Afternoon*, and Robert De Niro in *Taxi Driver*. All men. They experience life for the sake of experience. I want that, too. I want to live an exciting life, too.

After seeing Scorsese's *Taxi Driver*, I left the theater totally inspired by its grittiness. I am still in the movie. I am walking in slow motion. My eyes are the camera, slowly bobbing up and down, with the soundtrack of my footsteps clacking against the concrete pavement. New York City faces look into me and I shoot them in slow motion through my pretend lens.

Then, I am taken out of my delicious bubble by the asshole that says, "Baby you're good to look at!" I turn and try to hold his gaze but the "Baby, mmm, you're nice" makes me pull my eyes away, stung by that terrible discomfort lodged deep in my gut, like a claw, that only other women can comprehend. It's so hard to concentrate when you are prey for any Tom, Dick, or Harry.

Back to my film:

Focus—the bus pulling up, the doors opening with a phsssh as I get on, the driver's eyes never making contact with mine. I feel weird but I like it so I dwell in it. In my interior world I feel powerful, not like I felt with the guy on the street. I imagine turning the camera on myself as I take my seat and swirl my Guatemalan wool cape around for the visual effect. I know I am still in the movie so everything is dramatized for me. I take a seat and swing myself sideways so I can look out the window and watch the city go by. I fantasize photographs that I want to take in full color. I want to shoot *Taxi Driver*–like scenes— blood, black skin drenched in heavy sweat shining against orange buildings; whores' thighs pressed against cracked and peeling city stoops. I want to sink myself into what I don't know.

My attention diverts to a very attractive man on the bus. My camera eyes all of him, tall with tight muscular thighs and ass pushing against his tailored suit. He carries an expensive attaché case. I imagine taking him home and feeling him inside of me, his sweat against mine . . .

CUT

I arrive at my stop and step off the bus into the warm day. I cross the street to my building and see old women sitting and talking together on the stoop. As I pass them, we all warmly smile at each other. They smile because they see a seemingly nice girl; I smile because they could never imagine the girl that I am.

Yes, I sought the freedom and autonomy, like men, to think dirty, jagged thoughts, to be fierce and unconventional. This is who I wanted to be—perhaps an artist like James Dean, perhaps a dreamer, perhaps a dilettante. It didn't matter. I wanted to create my own experiences, my own life. It was 1976 and I was a woman; I wanted to have more choices—like the rebel James Dean. It was that desire to be recognized as a multidimensional person, as well as my displeasure at the lack of acknowledgment of women who did excel, that propelled me to want to open Sahara. It was an attempt to administer to the frustration of a large population of people who felt ignored and insignificant. Opening Sahara was an act of innocence and defiance.

•

A "night club created by women for women" read the invitation to our grand opening. No more hiding for us. Sahara opened on May 1, 1976, at 1234 Second Avenue where it intersects with East 65th Street. It was located in an Upper East Side neighborhood that Barbara called "Straightsville."

It was finally true. There would be no more shame, no more degradation for us. Adrienne, my college roommate, hand addressed the invitations for the opening, while trucks delivered huge palm trees to visually reinforce our desert theme. When the Italian couches arrived, our vision of elegance manifested itself in reality. Having spent a substantial amount on the impressive sound system, palm trees, and couches, our money had dwindled. Thank God for

1234 SECOND AVENUE AT 65 STREET

**THE FIRST NIGHT·CLUB
CREATED BY WOMEN FOR WOMEN**

**ANNOUNCES ITS OPENING
DATE: SAT, MAY 1 TIME: 9 P.M.**

WELCOME TO YOUR CLUB

$5.00 minimum

FIG. 14. Invitation to the opening of Sahara, 1976.

Barbara's family, some of whom worked in construction, who helped us build out the club for very little compensation.

All of our friends contributed in small but meaningful ways to the opening. Not only did Adrienne help address hundreds of invitations but she and Dotty labored away in the basement kitchen of the club making quiche to serve at the opening party. According to Adrienne, our greatest victory that night was that no one died from food poisoning.

Sahara was housed in a small two-story building. Behind a large picture window in the front of the building, cacti were planted in undulating layers of pink-, yellow-, and blue-colored sand, like a huge glass terrarium, to depict the "oasis in the desert" theme of the club. The large, custom wood carving of the name, "Sahara," with its distinctive logo created by Barbara's cousin, Peter Fodero, in a font that made the letters look like swaying palm trees amongst the dunes, rested on top of the sand in the window, creating a dramatically lit landscape. No detail was left to chance. The same logo was also emblazoned on the outside canopy leading into the club.

Success is often in the timing, and the timing was right for Sahara. The expressions on the faces of the women when they

FIG. 15. Front of Sahara, 1977. Photo credit: Beate Nilsen.

entered the club for the first time and were handed a rose were priceless. Gasps erupted from their mouths because what they were expecting was more of what they were used to, which was very little; instead, they were overwhelmed by the elegance they encountered. Depleted, minimal expectations had created a collective low self-esteem that Sahara was determined to correct.

I still remember every detail of the club. Along the left wall of the first-floor lounge was a long, butcher-block bar. The floor was

FIG. 16. A customer, Judi, by the front window of Sahara, 1977. Photo credit: Meryl Meisler, reprinted by permission.

covered in dark gray wall-to-wall carpeting and the room was furnished with contemporary Italian sectional couches covered in a soft, black, nubby fabric. Director's chairs and swaying palm trees surrounded round wooden tables. Large Bombay wicker fan chairs were placed in the corners of the room.

Huge contemporary paintings by women artists brought color and life to the intentionally beige walls. The art conveyed everything that the world needed to know about women: that we were

FIG. 17. Sahara owners and Alix inside Sahara, from left to right: Michelle, Alix, Linda, Barbara, and me.

extraordinary, talented, and not to be ignored. Directly ahead on the left was a small stage. Across from the stage was the stairway up to the second-floor disco.

The second story housed another long bar and the dance room, which boasted a state-of-the-art sound system and a DJ booth. Complemented by the rain lights throughout the room that pulsated beams of light onto the dance floor, along with other blinking colored lights that reflected off a mirrored ball hung from the ceiling, all of it was perfectly synchronized with the music.

Since the upstairs was separated by a stairwell to the lounge, the downstairs remained relatively quiet. You could have conversations or perhaps link up with someone you had never met before.

We wanted Sahara to be a place to party but also a place to connect.

·

I was thrilled when Beth came to the opening with the rest of our college friends. We all danced together in a circle. It was surreal to have Beth dancing in front of me again after all these years. In college, I couldn't admit to myself how attracted to her I was, but now I was different. I watched her dance with her eyes closed, knowing that she was feeling everything around her. I remembered her saying when we first met in college, "Everything in life is sensual to me—anything that has color, a smell, a texture, or a sound." To me, she emanated that sensuality from every pore of her body.

The opening was an enormous success. The accolades kept coming. "What a spectacular party," my friend Alix Kucker[1] whispered into my ear as she passed.

"Leslie, everyone's here! They're all stunning!" another woman said with a flirtatious squeeze on my arm.

The white, red, and purple lights illuminated all of the women's faces, while sweat dripped from their foreheads and seeped through their blouses. The deep pulse of the music had taken over every surface of the building. The walls shook and the floors bounced. Inside the newly built Sahara, our love for each other and ourselves was welcomed with a glorious sense of abandon and wide-open arms.

·

After the club opened, I quickly realized that I was being seduced by the nightlife—the women gathered together like a unique and solidifying tribe, a sea of bodies dancing together under the strobe lights. Disco music was the predominant soundtrack of the time. Music was everywhere in the club, playing in the background in our basement office and emanating from the jukebox in the lounge or the records being spun by the DJ in the upstairs discotheque. We danced for hours on end, united in mutual elation by the shared freedom and stoked libidos.

On the dance floor, my senses were always aroused. I detected other people's eyes on me because I was one of the owners, even when I closed my own to totally lose myself in the beats and the

FIG. 18. Me inside Sahara, obviously filled with the thrill of success. Photo credit: Sarah Lewis.

deep reverberations of the bass speakers entering my core. I relished the recognition and attention I received. I wanted my customers to know that I was part of them, equally in love with the moment, the music, and the frenzy of abandonment. Often, I played the tambourine and marimbas with a small group of women clustered together on the dance floor, jamming to the music blasting from the tweeters and bass speakers, a symphony conducted by the DJ from her booth.

The bartenders joined in the dancing from behind the bar; the sounds from the speakers ricocheted like bolts of lightning across the room, bouncing off the walls. The packed dance floor of women was driven wild with the cacophony of the loud pumping rhythms and the camaraderie that filled the air.

This was our club—*we created this*—and these jubilant participants were my extended family. Sahara was a primal manifestation of and reconnection to the most joyful parts of my childhood—being around the women in my family, music, and dance. Those things were the antidotes to my fears as a child, caused by a father who was deeply wounded and whose damage infected not only his own life but also that of his wife and children. This club was an extension of that antidote. On the dance floor, under the lights, I found my place in the world.

•

My choice to open a women's nightclub inevitably derailed my art career in New York. That was the price I chose to pay. Early in the process, I had abandoned my initial plan to get the club up and running and then look for another art job. I became enamored with the nightclub business—this extraordinary netherworld that operated completely outside the mainstream.

Although I didn't want to walk away from the art world, it was clear that I was not cut out to be an art history scholar. After all those years of study and hard work, I could see that there were many things I did not like or find fulfilling about it as a career. I loved art and being around creative people, but I didn't want to spend my time writing obscure treatises on art history minutiae, which was a requirement if I wanted to obtain and maintain a position in academia.

But what also propelled me to get more enmeshed in the club was that I had grown tired of working for other people. I had worked for the big guys, John Coplans at *Artforum* and Mario Amaya at the New York Cultural Center, stars in their own right. It was time for me to shine on my own. I was *finished* working with crazy people and their neuroses. I wanted to be my own boss and have other people deal with *my* neuroses!

Sahara offered me the opportunity to create something and get credit for it. I wanted to be acknowledged. You rarely receive credit for your achievements when you work for someone else, especially if you are a woman. Sahara offered me the opportunity to make a unique contribution to society at a time it was sorely needed. I didn't think I could provide something as important or worthwhile in the art world.

My involvement in the club grew immediately. I took a crash course in bartending and worked the weekday cocktail hours, 5:00 P.M. until 8:00 P.M. We were all so inexperienced that none of us had accounted for all the daytime work that owning a nightclub required. Originally, I would arrive at 4:00 P.M. to open the club and prep the bar, but those hours kept expanding as I realized there were a slew of daytime activities that had to be taken care of as well. Someone had to be there to accept deliveries and set up the bar. Some machine or strobe light was always breaking down and I had to make sure it was up and running when the sun set. I also worked Tuesday nights until closing at 4:00 A.M. as a bartender. Meanwhile, the phones never stopped ringing.

My partners worked the nights from Wednesday through Sunday. They ordered the liquor, managed the inventory, paid the bills and supervised the staff. Being up until all hours of the night operating the club was exhausting. Tired and coming down from their highs, my partners would leave me notes of what had to be handled the next day, confident that I would manage it.

Sahara became a blank canvas to create whatever I pleased, without anyone telling me what to do or how to do it. The workload grew exponentially as I began to see more and more opportunities to curate the club, making it an art gallery, political forum, and performance space. In addition to mounting changing art exhibitions, I spent hours scouting for musical acts and live performance events. I had to hang the art I curated and arrange rehearsals for the acts I scheduled. I also booked fashion shows, workshops, and political benefits.

The interaction of the art, music, fashion, and political events with the mostly female audience (who came from every possible walk of life), and the way they responded to it, became a conceptual art piece in and of itself for me. There is a subtle transformation of taste that occurs when one is constantly exposed to outstanding art regardless of whether the art is understood or not. The art at Sahara[2] was absorbed subcutaneously by the women who came to the club, no matter their economic, social, or cultural backgrounds. It imbued them and the club with a sense of the exceptional. On more than one occasion, I overheard patrons say disparaging things like, "Oh please, a kid could do that." But as they lived with the art surrounding them in the club environment and our ever-changing exhibits became the norm, the comments became softer and more appreciative of the art's sophistication. "I don't know what the fuck you're hanging, but I can't believe I'm starting to like it!" said a woman standing in front of an early Louise Fishman piece hanging on the wall, which was simply a minimalist slab of plywood painted gray.

The woman's candor confirmed my intuition: mixing highbrow and lowbrow in our club erased the deceit and illuminated the contradictions inherent in these cultural divisions. Highbrow art, or fine art, as it's usually called, was created in the past for educated elites. Meanwhile, lowbrow art, or art with mass appeal, was made for the working classes. But not at Sahara. At the club, those distinctions melted away. There was no division of cultures between low and high. Culture was culture and everyone joined in and was part of it. I loved that, not only because a mixture of the philistine and refined appealed to the diversity of my own nature but also because Sahara felt like an encapsulation of the contradictions of life itself. I'm sure it was the same for others. I exalted in the joy of my own self-actualization and the

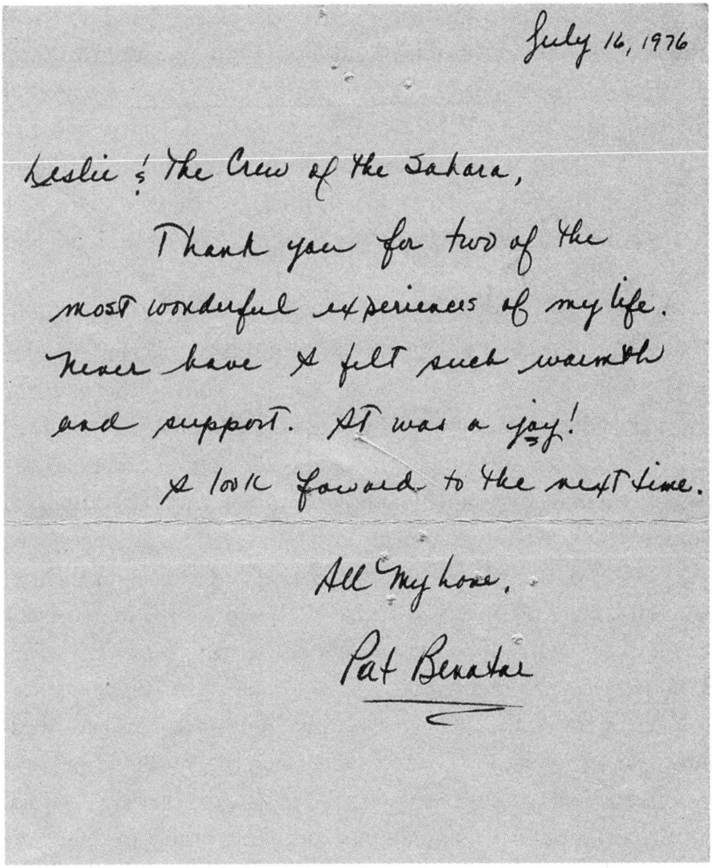

July 16, 1976

Leslie & The Crew of the Sahara,

Thank you for two of the most wonderful experiences of my life. Never have I felt such warmth and support. It was a joy!

I look forward to the next time.

All my love,

Pat Benatar

FIG. 19. Pat Benatar letter.

idea that I helped create and foster this new awareness of art in others.

•

I started a live music night every week called "Thursdays at Sahara" and began to book talent. This was the only night that men were allowed into the club. Pat Benatar was the second act I booked. My brother saw her at Catch a Rising Star, a local comedy club, and flipped out for her. She then auditioned at Sahara and I hired her. Pat and her band became our most frequently recurring act.

Holly Woodlawn and Jackie Curtis, the underground transvestite legends immortalized by Andy Warhol in his films *Trash* and *Flesh*, performed. Nona Hendryx appeared, as well as so many other amazing performers. Whatever free nights I had, I spent going to talent showcases at other clubs to look for acts to book for Thursday nights. It didn't take long for "Thursdays at Sahara" to become a tremendous success and legendary for the diverse crowd it brought into the club.

Expanding our audiences on Thursday nights was important to me because I wanted to increase the visibility of the club, to educate the heterosexual world, both men and women, that lesbians existed in all shapes and sizes. I wanted to extinguish the ingrained false notions and stereotypes that had made homosexuality anathema. I thought that if men could see women through a different lens, without the obfuscation of power and sex fogging their view, they would have a whole new appreciation and respect for them as human beings. We even advertised "Thursdays at Sahara" every week in the mainstream downtown newspaper, *The Village Voice*. And people came in droves.

We operated the club on two divergent principles. We were always combating the dilemma and tension that resulted from trying to balance the desire to protect our lesbian clientele's privacy while, at the same time, making them more visible to the world and, therefore, hopefully acceptable. It was difficult because women were very frightened at that time, and reasonably so, of having their sexual orientation discovered and losing their jobs or, worse, their children and families. We were forced to walk a very fine tightrope between protection and visibility.

10

An Antidote to Boredom

Not long after Sahara opened, my friend Dotty called to tell me that Beth and Steven were moving to Woodstock, New York. I called Beth to find out if this was true.

"Yes, we are moving to Woodstock," Beth confirmed.

"Upstate New York, really?" I said.

"Yes, it's better for Steven. He can find better antiques up there to sell," she said.

"Do you want to move? I thought you liked being in the city."

She said, "I do want to go, if it will make it easier for Steven. I also love being in the country, so I'm sure it will be fine."

"It'll be wonderful. Beautiful and tranquil. I'm happy for you, but I'll miss you," I responded.

"I'll miss you, too. Les, you just have to promise me that you won't let another ten years go by without us seeing each other. Will you promise to visit, once we get settled?"

"Sure," I said. "I would love to."

And then she was gone. As quickly as she had reentered my life, she left.

•

In the meantime, there were three attractive, apparently affluent women from the suburbs who started to frequent Sahara for cocktail hour. Since I was the only bartender, and the club was virtually empty at cocktail hour, we got to know each other well. Their names were Brooke, Elaine, and Trudie. They were married, mothers, and best friends. They laughed at each other's every word. There was mischief in their eyes. They always arrived at the club in a stretch limousine that bore a personalized license plate that read "Trudie G" and had the driver wait outside the bar for them.

Elaine and Brooke were now in a relationship with each other and Trudie was their sidekick, but she had also slept with each of them at different times in the past. They had all met at swinger parties, those rowdy, group, pre-AIDS sex romps of the 1970s, with their husbands. Although they were still married at the time they started coming to Sahara, at some point shortly thereafter they realized they were gay. Their marriages fell apart, they divorced their husbands, and then they started coming to Sahara more frequently and at night.

Brooke took a liking to me and Elaine to Carolee, who I was still dating at the time, although our relationship was on the wane. Eventually, we just switched partners, like a do-si-do at a square dance: I started dating Brooke and Carolee started dating Elaine. Brooke and I spent the next few months together. Often, I would spend a weekend night at her large house in New Jersey with her and her three young children. Sometimes, after a weeknight at Sahara, not wanting to travel back to New Jersey, Brooke would book a room at the Plaza Hotel and I would join her there after work. We were having fun together, but I did not want it to go any further.

•

There is only so much one can do in a nightclub waiting for the hours to pass. When the party is happening and everything is in full swing—the bars going strong, the music blasting away, and the crowd left to its own devices—how does a club owner pass the time? At Sahara, I would leave the basement office and go upstairs to check the bars, bring change to the bartenders, and make sure there were enough lemons to slice. Then, I danced. I would worry about running out of ice and call Brusca, the iceman, to bring over bags because the ice machine couldn't produce enough to keep up with the volume of drinks. Or, when I needed quarters,

I ran next door to the all-night coffee shop, the Silver Star, and begged them to give us some of theirs.

I broke up the occasional fight and made sure the lighting was just right and that the music was bringing people onto the dance floor. Then, I danced a little more. I would go into the DJ booth and run the disco lights, flicking different switches on and off, each program providing different pulsating lighting effects and patterns that could change the atmosphere of the room and the mood of the crowd in seconds. Sometimes, I would grab the tambourine from behind the bar and play along with other girls hitting their tambourines on the dance floor. Other times, when it was really crowded, I would jump behind the bar to help an overwhelmed bartender pour more drinks. Or I would scurry around, cleaning ashtrays and picking up empty glasses when it was impossible for the waitresses to handle it all. But mostly, I mingled with customers. They were always very excited to see me, with big kisses and hugs, as if I hadn't seen them in months, even though it was likely that I had just seen them a few nights before. But any real conversation was impossible because the music was very loud, so we would nod at each other, pretending to understand what the other person was saying through their facial expressions until someone gave up and said, "Music's too loud! I can't hear you!" Another kiss and hug good-bye and then I would move on to the next person and repeat the same routine . . . and so on and so forth, over and over again.

•

We spent some part of every night downstairs in the basement office, our sanctuary, doing drugs or watching others do drugs to help pass the time and heighten the camaraderie between whoever was there. Drugs, especially cocaine, were ubiquitous. Drugs were our antidote to boredom. Snorting cocaine was not only a social ritual among many clubgoers and workers but a way to stay up and not crash in the wee hours of the morning. Cocaine kept you pumped, chatty and interactive.

My partners had started to talk about someone named Kay Santiago: "You've got to meet Kay"; "maybe Kay can cover for so and so"; or "will Kay be here tonight?" I wondered "Who is this Kay and why is she so important to them?"

I soon found out. Kay was an overweight, heavily freckled, red-headed Puerto Rican who grew up in a government housing project in the tough neighborhood of the South Bronx. She was the epitome of "street" and one of the coolest chicks you'd ever meet. She had this laid-back, self-assured demeanor. She never imposed herself. Instead, she just waited for you to come to her, and everyone did.

She had been an embalmer before she lost her job and became a full-time drug dealer. No matter what other, more legal endeavors she tried in an effort to stop dealing, she could never get them off the ground. Drug dealing was truly her forte, and because of who she was, and my partners' penchant for cocaine, she became one of their closest friends, and eventually one of mine.

My introduction to Kay occurred one night when I was hanging out at the upstairs bar. Joey (Joanne) Mano was the bartender that night and her moll-like girlfriend, Jackie, was parked in her usual spot on the barstool at the corner of the bar. We called them Mr. and Mrs. Mano way before gay marriage was a feasible reality. Joey was a handsome, androgynous lesbian, and Jackie was what would later be referred to as a "lipstick lesbian."[1] Jackie had perfectly manicured long red nails and matching painted red lips. Like a 1950s pinup girl, she perched on the barstool with her long legs crossed and exposed, dressed in a tight skirt, stockings with straight seams running up the back, and very high-heeled shoes, which clearly enhanced her shapely legs. She smoked cigarettes continuously, one after the other, filling the ashtray with her signature lipstick-rimmed cigarette butts, and from her vantage point surveyed the room and kept an eye on Joey.

Jackie and Joey were both New Jersey girls and had the accents to prove it. Jackie liked antagonizing Joey by openly flirting with Michelle, who was always hiding from Joey because she thought Joey would kill her. Anyway, the night I met Kay, I was at the other end of the bar when I noticed her standing next to Jackie in the corner. I knew who she was but we had not formally met. I was

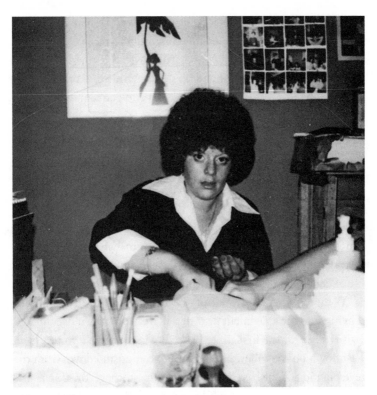

FIG. 20. Kay in Sahara's office.

watching the dance floor when Joey approached me from behind the bar, tapped me on the shoulder, and, when I turned around discreetly, put a joint in my hand, pointing at Kay. I looked up and nodded to her to acknowledge the gift and Kay nodded back. No words spoken—very cool. That was our first encounter, which ultimately turned into a long and close friendship.

•

The small apartment building next door to Sahara housed the Silver Star coffee shop on its ground floor. We had already grown quite close to Gus, the heavyset, middle-aged Greek owner, and his staff because so many of our customers patronized his coffee shop. One night he stopped by the club to tell me, in his heavy Greek accent, that we had a problem. He said that one of his tenants was complaining about the noise from the club. Despite the expensive soundproofing we had installed in order to receive the zoning variance from the city, the sound still traveled through the walls to Gus's tenant's apartment and was making his life miserable. To alleviate the problem, Gus said, "We have to get him out. Do you know anyone who might want to live there?"

Our new friend, Kay, still lived in the Bronx, but we knew she desperately wanted to move to the city. She was the perfect solution to our dilemma because we needed someone in the apartment who kept our hours; that was no problem for Kay, who rarely seemed to sleep. Instead, sitting like a Buddha statue, she would nod off for minutes at a time, at any time of the day or night, sometimes mid-conversation with someone, until she suddenly realized she had fallen asleep, jerked herself awake, snorted another hit of cocaine, and continued the conversation.

We were Kay's ticket out of the Bronx. Kay loved the idea of moving into the apartment next to Sahara. After she moved in and I visited her for the first time, I asked to use her bathroom. When I sat down on the toilet, I literally bounced up and down from the reverberation of the bass speakers pounding through the thin apartment walls from the club while I nervously watched her toiletries rattle precariously on the glass shelves next to her sink. From then on, Kay's bathroom became known as the "boom-boom room."

Kay's apartment became the refuge we escaped to after work and on our nights off. There was always an endless supply of cocaine sitting in a bowl in the middle of a large round coffee table in the living room, with an incongruous mix of friends, acquaintances, celebrities, and models, rich and poor, sitting on the floor around the table, partaking of her largesse. We joked that it was a great place to bring a date on Saturday night.

Everyone adored Kay, not only because she was inherently generous, powerful, and charismatic but also incredibly indifferent to status. She treated everyone the same no matter who they were. She spoke her street lingo and said fuck you to anyone she felt like, regardless of who they were. She would introduce her new celebrity friends to the tough Latin guys that she grew up with in the projects. They were Kay's security, and they watched her back and hung out at her apartment with everyone else. She used cocaine as an entrée into the lives of the rich and famous, who were totally fascinated by her perilous yet titillating world. They found it sexy, as danger can be.

All her friends became "Kay groupies," sitting around the table, engaged in that intense, seemingly profound coke dialogue that meanders endlessly and goes nowhere. Kay offered the wealthy and prominent a respite from their high-ranking pretensions. It was fun to watch them in action with her, so solicitous and subservient in contrast to their upbringing—bowing, straightening up her apartment, scurrying around, serving her guests. In the end, Kay probably gave away more coke than she ever sold because she never liked to blow alone.

A lot of influential people became her customers. She was the Godmother—our protector, if ever there was a need. She was a drug dealer with a heart of gold, helping the down-and-out, doing deals with a handshake, getting screwed out of money, and planning revenge. She was both angel and devil incarnate.

·

There was often some insane event at Sahara that made us laugh so hard we cried. But especially on Thursday nights, with the live acts, you never knew what to expect. One particular night stands out because it really demonstrated the breadth of our audience.

On this night, the club was filling up fast for the show. The bartenders were working frantically, turning out drinks as if they were on an assembly line. The waitresses were pushing their way through the crowd, trays filled with drinks balanced precariously over their heads. When the entertainment arrived, we shepherded them downstairs to the office to dress and prepare for their show.

In the office, the activity became nearly as hectic as upstairs. The act prepared to go on. The female singer was now half-dressed, touching up her makeup and discussing cues with her band, while the club staff and other assorted people filtered in and out of the office, barely noticing her. All sense of propriety was gone because there was just not enough space to be modest.

Behind all this activity was the din of the customers and the music upstairs, mixed with the sound of clanking pipes from behind the walls and water running through them like a stream through the office. Michelle and I sat behind our desks stacked high with papers. I was writing reminders to myself in a spiral notebook.

The phones always rang nonstop. We robotically answered these calls because the questions were repetitively the same.

"Yes, 1234 Second Avenue—65th Street and Second Avenue . . ."

"No, she's not working tonight . . ."

"The show starts at eleven . . ."

"Yes, the disco opens after the show . . ."

"Yes, men are allowed if they're accompanied by women, but make sure they're well-behaved and respectful."

Occasionally, if the phone was picked up at the upstairs bar, we might hear a knock on the pipes, our makeshift intercom system, which signaled something important that needed our attention, so we would pick up the phone downstairs in the office.

I looked at the clock. It was 11:00 P.M. I turned to the singer: "Figure that you'll go on around 11:20 P.M.—give everyone some extra time to settle in."

It was 11:10 when I told the band I was going upstairs and instructed them: "At 11:15, 11:20, come wait by the bathrooms and I'll announce you."

Each Thursday night was filled with anticipation: Is it going to be a good night? Will we be crowded? Will they like the show? Are we going to make money?

•

The upstairs was jam-packed on this night. I pushed my way through the crowd and called out to Michelle, "Okay, I think we're ready." I looked at the girl behind the bar and yelled over the crowd, "Kill the house lights when you see me onstage."

The girl couldn't hear me, so I repeated it louder. "Kill the house lights when you see me go up on the stage. Do you know how?"

She answered, "I think so."

Frustrated, I said, "Would you PLEASE learn how to do it?"

Michelle saw that I was rattled, and said, "Go ahead. I'll do it."

I made my way through the crowd, saw the band waiting to go on, and gave them a nod. After they took their places on the small stage, they began to tune their instruments—you could hear the sounds of tightening guitar strings being plucked and drumsticks beating on the snare and cymbals while the foot pedal banged against the bass drum—the preparatory, musical discord that suggested what was to come. I stepped up onto the stage and signaled Michelle; the stage lights went on, the house lights came down. I looked out at the darkened room filled with women and some men, took a deep breath to calm my nerves, and turned on the microphone. "Good evening ladies and gentlemen. Welcome to Sahara. Would you please join me in giving a warm welcome to Pat Benatar?"

•

After the show, the disco opened, and we returned to the office to pay the act. That night, Paulette, who worked the front door collecting admissions, frantically called downstairs. We could tell it was an emergency from the hyper, machine gun–like way she fired off clipped words when she was nervous. It was hard to understand her, but we somehow deciphered that there was a problem at the door. I rushed upstairs to see three beefy guys talking heatedly to Duane, our bouncer, who was an off-duty cop. Paulette and Duane were both trying to block these guys from entering the club. One of them turned out to be someone's husband looking for his errant wife. His two friends were there as his backup.

"I know she's in there! Let me in!" The man was loud and drawing the attention of the customers inside.

I approached him and gently said, "Please calm down, sir. We want to help you. Who are you looking for?" When he said his wife's name, we immediately knew who she was and that she was inside the club. I said, "Let me see if she's here. But please, you must wait at the door. If I find her, I will bring her to you. I promise. Just wait here."

He calmed down and agreed. We then rushed around, frantically looking for her, knowing that when we found her, we'd hide her. I finally spotted her dancing in the disco, pressed up against another woman, lost in the music. I broke in to tell her that her husband was there looking for her. She immediately panicked and let us hide her in the fire exit stairwell leading down from the disco to the street. We returned to her irate husband and his pals, telling them we couldn't find her, but that if they would like to check for themselves, we would be happy to accommodate them. We accompanied them as they searched the club, and only after they realized it was fruitless did they decide to leave.

"Whew. That was close!" I said to the others with a smile and returned to my business in the office. Not until the end of the night, hours later when the disco had cleared out, did we hear muffled cries from the stairwell and realize the errant wife was still locked in there.

•

Winding up the night, the bartenders would yell out in singsong: "Last call . . . for alcoholllll. . . ." Duane would usher out the last customers. The bartenders would close out their registers and come down to the office with their money and register tapes stuffed into the large metal cups used to mix drinks and hand them, one by one, over to Michelle or me to tally and balance the proceeds against the tapes.

When they were finished, the staff would go upstairs to sit around together in the dark lounge and chill out. By this time, it would be 5:00 A.M. After we were done, Michelle and I would join them to decompress from the night, with just the bar and jukebox lights on, drinking and sharing joints. The room would still be smoky, with cigarette butts all over the floor and half-filled cocktail glasses and dirty ashtrays scattered all around, like the detritus of a playing (in our case pleasure) field after a game. The place would smell of stale booze and cigarettes from deep within the carpet and couches.

We would all smell of it, too. We would sit slouched against each other, listening to the stories about things that happened that night. Kay once told the story of how she was forced to become a bartender at Sahara. She said, "I went to the bar one night. Barbara

FIG. 21. Sahara staff at the upstairs bar; we had a great crew working for us.

and Linda were in a panic because Judy, the bartender, just got 'married' and went off to Jersey with her new wife. . . ." She took a toke off a joint, passed it to Michelle, and continued. "And Vicki, the other bartender, had just died in a car accident . . ."

One of the staff said, "That was so horrible."

We all nodded sadly in agreement. Kay continued, "Jamie 'Slick,' another bartender, got *too* slick, went on vacation, and the girls never let her back in." Everyone laughed as Michelle and I nodded to one another in acknowledgment. "So, on the spot, because they had no one else, they made me *head* bartender, except, because I'm a Rican, all I know how to make is rum and coke!"

"Oh no," exclaimed another one of the staff slouched down on the couch across from us. We were all laughing.

Kay continued, "I lasted three months only because I went on black beauties. And I lost more money than I made because I couldn't deal coke. 'Go to bartending school,' they told me. Lasted one fucking day. The teacher gave me a crash course of fucking life, man. Suddenly I'm the head bartender and I don't know what the fuck I'm doing."

I interjected, "I can't figure out why you wanted to hang out with us in the first place. You probably thought that we could lead you to a good psychotherapist, because you obviously needed one."

Kay responded, "Where I come from the only therapy I know is homicide or suicide."

Michelle said, "Very funny, but true."

Kay said, "All I know is I go home, and my mother says, 'You've got a new language—schlepping, schvitzing, schmuck? What's the matter with you?' I tell her that's who I hang out with now—Jews." She paused a moment, then added, "It's not the fucking Mafia so she's happy."

Michelle chimed in, "What do you think *my* mother thinks when I start repeating what my friend has taught me, like, 'I'm gonna cut you high, wide, and deep.' My mother is thrilled with my new friends."

Kay was not deterred, "My family wonders why I hang out at this place, Sahara, all the time. They think Sahara is a pawnshop, a fence, a rehab center, or a drug depot." Kay laughed. "Yesterday my cousin called and ordered a VCR and then, when I freaked out, you all wondered why! You white girls are gonna' kill me."

•

We had all survived another night, some more laughs, and some more heartache. The staff would drag their tired asses home and were back the next night fresh and ready to repeat it all again. It is unimaginable how the club ever came together and ended up presentable every day, but sure enough, Chen, our porter, would scour, dust, and vacuum the grime away so that it was clean and ready by opening time. The scars of cigarette burns in the carpet, the rips in the upholstery, and the scratches on the walls would somehow be hidden in the darkness of the dimmed lighting. So bring on the women, the music, the joy, and the sadness all over again—we were ready.

That's why we were all so close. The club was our shared cocoon. We were living our nocturnal lives together within that space and what went on beyond its walls was ancillary. The outside world didn't exist. That's why exiting the club at the end of a long night was so jarring. We were once again confronted by the real world. There was no way to prepare yourself for the palpable physical reaction you experienced when the door was opened after you'd spent many hours in a dark, smoke-filled room. The bright glare of a new day's sun would hit you smack in the eyes. The sunlight, the fresh air, the noise and traffic rumbling like the sound of a train down Second Avenue, the hustle and bustle of people rushing to work like lemmings to the sea would all hit you with a sensory overload of discordant sights and sounds. You would instinctively raise your hands to cover your eyes and shield yourself from the onslaught until you were able to adjust.

There was always a small cab line waiting outside the club for customers, and the drivers were familiar with the staff. We would put Michelle, who by this time would be so stoned she would be walking precariously off balance and slurring her words, into a taxi. Harold, one of the regular cabbies who knew Michelle well, would say, "Don't worry. I'll take care of her." Someone would joke, "How does Michelle hail a cab at night?" We would all answer in unison, "*She falls in front of it.*" We would say our good-byes. It was reassuring to know that they'd all get home safely.

11

Permission

Toward the end of that first summer at Sahara, the club was in full swing and we were working day and night. We were very successful; our hopes and dreams were all being actualized. I desperately needed a break for a few days, away from the club and the soot, heat, noise, and stress of New York City. Beth's invitation to visit her in Woodstock was becoming more and more attractive and I wanted to see her, so I suggested to Brooke that we go upstate to see my college friend. I called Beth to ask if her offer was still on the table.

Eagerly, Beth said, "Absolutely! I'm so happy you called. I'm so excited. We have some other friends coming up to visit that weekend, but we'll set them up somewhere else."

I was surprised that she would relocate her other friends so quickly just for us. "Are you sure? We could come another time," I said.

She insisted, "No. Don't worry. I want to see you. They'll stay someplace else."

So, Brooke and I made the two-hour drive to Woodstock. I told Brooke that Beth was a very special friend from college and I looked forward to introducing her to Beth and her boyfriend, Steven. I did not mention my deeper feelings for Beth, only that I was very eager to see her again. Inside, I was nervous with anticipation, not knowing what to expect or how it would be staying with Beth and Steven for the weekend. I made Brooke listen to jazz in the car, even though she preferred disco, to help me relax. As the greenery of the countryside started to appear and the concrete faded in my rearview mirror, I started to calm down.

Finally, we found their small red house at the end of a winding country road. Beth and Steven rushed out to greet us. Beth introduced me to Steven, I introduced them both to Brooke, and we all embraced. The setting was charming. Entering, I could see straight through the glass sliding doors at the rear of the house to the pool overlooking a magnificently wide-open vista of lush green valley and mountains. "Oh, this is perfect!" I exclaimed as I rushed outside to take it all in. Beth and Brooke followed me out.

I was so hungry for fresh air and nature's glory that the onslaught of color, cleanliness and fragrant smells overwhelmed me. As if I had decompressed too quickly from the city's dirt and hardness, feeling like a wild child freed from its lair, my modesty evaporated on the spot and I impulsively pulled off my top to let the sweet country air caress and permeate my skin. I spread my arms wide, closed my eyes and took a slow, deep breath to fill my lungs. As I exhaled, I let go a deep sigh of relief. I turned and saw Beth observing my nakedness and our eyes met for a moment. I knew she, my sensual confidante, would understand the joy and serenity that swept over me at that moment. It was so good to see her again.

The four of us shared a bottle of wine and talked about Steven's antique business and how different it was living in Woodstock compared to New York City. At the end of the evening, Brooke and I went to our room. The room showed Beth's imprint—it was simple, shabby chic, yet casually elegant. Every detail was attended to. The different patterns of the throw pillows and the comforter played harmoniously off each other, with shades of color in the comforter picking up a subtle color in the pillows and rug. The color scheme was calm and soothing. Brooke and I didn't talk much, tired after the long drive and a little too much wine. It was just as well because my thoughts were of Beth.

The next day was sunny, and Steven left the house in the afternoon to play basketball with his friends, leaving Brooke, Beth, and me to hang out. Brooke and I each swallowed a quaalude and Beth was drinking tequila, so we were all very relaxed and enjoying each other's company. I was so glad to be away from the city. We were lounging in the living room, sharing our stories, when Brooke casually asked, "Beth, have you ever thought of sleeping with a woman?" Whoa, I thought to myself. Did she really just ask her that?

Forthright as always, Beth answered with ease, "Yes, I have fantasized about being with a woman, but have never acted on it."

Taken aback, I didn't know how to react to her answer, so I remained silent.

"That's interesting," Brooke said.

Beth continued. "Steven and I even discussed it. He's very secure in his masculinity. He's not threatened by the idea at all," she said, talking to both of us at the same time. Then she said, "He's even encouraged me to try it, to see what it's like. He finds it provocative, like most men, I guess," she said as I averted my eyes from hers.

I sat very quietly and listened, not saying a word. I did not want to convey any hint of anticipation or sexual desire, but my quaalude was beginning to kick in. I noticed that Beth's lips were so full they looked swollen, as if they had been kissed repeatedly for too long. They had this messy allure. Her upper lip did not have a clear beginning or end, the reddened pigment ending beyond its upper fold, like a river that overflowed its banks.

The quaaludes and tequila were apparently bringing out a laissez-faire attitude in all of us. Brooke, who was always game for a sexual adventure, asked, "Why haven't you tried it with Leslie? Since you're such good friends?" I was so dumbfounded by the exchange that I didn't know if I should run away or jump for joy.

Beth hesitantly looked at Brooke and then at me and said, "I don't know."

It was incredible to me that this conversation was taking place in front of me. I was a bystander, but I could not have been happier or more surprised at what was transpiring. As the effects of the quaalude continued to intensify, my sense of boundaries and propriety dissipated. That pill was truly an aphrodisiac. I couldn't control myself any longer. I had to feel Beth close to me. Finally, glassy-eyed, I looked over at her and asked, "Could I just hold you?" It might have sounded calculating, a pretense for having sex, but the physical closeness was truly all that I desired. We were already sacrosanct to each other so that's how my question emerged—as a sacred wish.

She smiled. "Yes, of course." She extended her hand. "Come with me."

I took Beth's hand and let her lead me up the stairs to her bedroom.

I looked back at Brooke from the stairwell as she nodded her acquiescence. She had initiated it, so she was, perhaps naively, fine with it. I watched Beth close the door gently behind us. She pulled the pretty comforter down. As we removed our shoes and settled in together on the bed, with our heads resting on the pillows and facing each other, she unexpectedly kissed me.

Surprised at her assertiveness, I returned the kiss and we began to make love, stripping away each layer of clothing until we lay bare. Her hands were soft and intentional. I loved her gentle scent. Our bodies were comfortable together, as if they had finally found where they belonged. Afterward, we lay wrapped in each other's arms.

Beth startled me when she suddenly sat up. She whispered, "I hear Steven downstairs."

I also heard him, and then him and Brooke laughing and making their way up the stairs to join us. That was usually the way Brooke and I operated, but not this time.

"I hope they're not coming in here expecting a scene?" I said to Beth, apprehensively.

"Me too," she said, gathering up her clothes.

I followed her lead. Steven entered first, with Brooke close behind. It was obvious they wanted to participate, but we wanted no part of it. Brooke and Steven both presumptuously sat down on the bed, but Beth and I quickly got up and, without saying a word, pulled on our clothes and left them there bewildered, staring at us as we exited the room. We went downstairs, sat on the couch in the living room with our arms around each other, and, frankly, did not care about what was going on upstairs.

The next morning Brooke and I drove back to the city together, but I was not mentally there with her. As she made small talk throughout the two-hour drive, I heard sounds emanating from her lips but could not make out the words. I was in some kind of parallel universe containing only Beth and me. Generous, loving Brooke—I cared deeply for her, but I think she already sensed that she had lost me to Beth.

•

At first it was hard being back in New York City at Sahara. Suddenly, the disco hits seemed overly loud and repetitive with too much pounding bass. But soon I slid back into the grind. There was always so much to do. I thought of calling Beth a few times, but decided it was useless. Silence would give us both time to clear our heads and put our experience together in its proper perspective.

A week later, I received a card from her in the mail. Inside, it said:

> Because of your being, your sensitivity, and your openness, I
> have now traveled through one of my fantasies. Our friendship,
> because of this tender sharing, has become deeper and of great
> meaning to me . . . I thank you . . .
>
> I love you . . .

A flood of emotions washed over me. I was so touched by her words. What happened between us was extraordinary, but I was fully aware of the realities: she was straight and I was gay; she lived in Woodstock and I lived in New York City. Maybe she trusted me with this intimate experience because I was a close friend, but to her it was still a novelty and nothing more than that. Maybe I was merely a vehicle for Beth to expand her own definition of herself. Whatever it was for her, I was grateful for the physical distance that separated us. I calmed myself, knowing that nothing further could develop. We would both get on with our lives. I would not expose myself to the pain of another Suri and the unbearable heartbreak of loving another woman who did not want to share her life with me because I, too, was a woman.

•

And we did get on with our lives. Beth and I didn't talk after I received her card, but a few months later, Dotty called with some news.

"You'll never guess . . ." she said, anxious to tell me.

"What can't I guess?" I interrupted.

"Beth is moving back to the city. She's going to stay with me for a while until she finds an apartment for her and Steven."

I couldn't hold back and yelled, "*What? You're kidding!*"

"Steven's going to travel back and forth between the city and the country to look for furniture to sell. Isn't that great? We can all spend time together again," Dotty said.

"It's wonderful," I said to Dotty, as I thought to myself, "Now, I'm fucked!"

I knew I was in love with her and had been from the moment we met again after all those years. The only thing that had kept me emotionally safe from her was the distance between us. How would I handle Beth staying at Dotty's apartment, which was just around the corner from mine?

•

The day Steven dropped Beth off at Dotty's apartment I was there, anxiously awaiting her arrival. When the door opened, she walked in with Steven, who was carrying her suitcase. We all hugged and said how glad we were to see each other again. But the attraction between Beth and me was palpable. To camouflage, Beth looked at Dotty, and I kept my attention on Steven. Finally, Steven said his good-byes and left to return to Woodstock. I was relieved to see him go. As I turned to look at her, there was an intensity between us that unnerved me. Something was transpiring that neither one of us could ignore.

Shortly thereafter, she came to my apartment alone and we made love again. We were clearly crazy about each other. It happened so quickly, like lightning. The next week, October 20, 1976, was Adrienne's birthday, and she invited Beth, Steven, Brooke, and me to her party, along with a bunch of our other friends. I was already vulnerable. Beth's relationship with Steven was much more serious than mine with Brooke, and I could not bear to witness it. When Beth and I were alone, I asked her something that I should not have but had to.

"Would you mind *not* bringing Steven to Adrienne's party? I know it's a selfish, ludicrous thing to request, and I have no right to ask it, but I am asking anyway because I don't think I can handle it."

"Will you bring Brooke?" Beth asked.

"Yes . . . I know it's not fair, but Brooke is more like a friend to me. We don't live together. We're not in a committed relationship like you . . ."

She interrupted, "I understand. I won't bring him."

The night of the party, I wore tight French jeans and a bold, striped, navy-and-white blazer that Brooke had given me. I knew I looked good. Adrienne lived in a walk-up building in the East 70s. By the time Brooke and I had climbed the three flights of stairs, my heart was racing and my body was palpitating in the anticipation of seeing Beth again. I knocked on the door and Adrienne opened it. I hugged her and wished her a happy birthday. Then I moved past her, searching the faces of the people gathered in the small living room. Brooke and I were stopped by an acquaintance who wanted to congratulate me on the club, but I was not paying attention. My senses were straining to hear Beth's voice, to smell her scent, to see her face.

Was she in the bedroom that was separated from the living room by a small walk-through kitchen? I couldn't observe her, but I just knew she was there. I could tangibly feel her, and I knew she could feel me as well, as if our hearts were connected by strings pulling us irretrievably towards each other. Then she walked into the living room and our eyes met. All else faded. We were undeniably in love. October 20, 1976, was the night we knew there was no turning back.

•

From that day on, Beth and I spent all of our free time together. We knew we were in the thick of it. The glorious discovery and the maelstrom of love enveloped us so quickly that we felt like horses thundering out of the gate after being restrained for too long. We simply could not pull ourselves apart. Our bodies and minds were so tightly wrapped around each other, spiraling together, it was as if we were caught in the funnel of a tornado. Shamelessly, Beth and I started to see each other whenever Steven was traveling upstate. We'd steal any moments we could—an hour here, a few hours there.

On the November day that I asked Beth to meet me at a restaurant near Sahara, Channel 5 News had warned that it would get down to twenty-four degrees. When she arrived, her frigid nose was red, but her green eyes danced like the lights in Times Square. As we sat facing each other, we held hands across the table as if we were the only two people on earth. Suddenly, I became quiet.

"What's wrong?" Beth asked.

I pulled myself closer to her and took a deep breath and said, "I'm in love with you. I know this with unfathomable certainty. You are the only one for me."

She looked deeply into my eyes and said, "And I am mad for you. I cannot bullshit myself about this. I'm flying when I'm with you."

I continued, "Listen, I can understand if being in a relationship with a woman would be too difficult for you, too much of a change, and you don't want to pursue this any further."

Her eyes filled with tears as she said, "Are you crazy?"

I said, "I know you care deeply for Steven and don't want to hurt him. I don't want this to end, but, if you can't handle it, it's better to tell me, *now*, while our relationship is still young, so there's less devastation. It's new so I'll still be able to handle it, but if it goes on much longer . . ."

She wiped her eyes and said, "I'm in love with you. I never felt like I owned my life until I met you. There's something so different about falling in love with a woman. It's supposedly a bad thing, but it feels like I'm claiming my life again."

I could feel the weight of what she was going through, just by her attempt to explain. The waiter approached our table but when he saw the intensity of the conversation, he discreetly walked away.

I said, "For me, I already know that I want to grow old with you."

Beth did not flinch. "Les, I do not fully understand what's going on, but I know that we are destined to be together. I just need some time. Can you give me that?"

I didn't know what that meant. Time—such a nebulous construct. How much time? What would I be doing while giving her time? But I nodded, yes. We barely touched the food we had ordered, leaving the restaurant knowing so much more, and less, than we had before.

•

One night, about two weeks after Beth and I met at the restaurant, she called. "I need to come over," she said excitedly into the phone.

"Sure. Come over." I was deeply curious to hear what she had to say.

When she arrived, we kissed deeply and held each other in a long embrace. We walked into my living room. Beth let her shoes drop to the floor as she sat cross-legged across from me on my couch. Grover Washington Jr.'s album *Mister Magic* was playing in the background. We began to drink from a bottle of Amaretto I had opened. She was all aglow, her eyes twinkling as she leaned in and kissed me. I waited patiently to hear what she had to say.

"I have something to tell you and it's wonderful. I decided to tell Steven about us."

"*What!*" My mouth fell open.

"Les, I couldn't stand deceiving him any longer. You know, truth is one of my ground rules. This lying was eating me up. I had to tell him. I talked to him and . . ."

"You told him we were *sleeping together*?"

"Yes, but I have great news," she said enthusiastically.

"What?" I said.

"Well, he was furious at first, but when I told him that I was unwilling to give you up, he finally agreed to let me see you. We can be together. I no longer have to lie. Isn't that fantastic?"

She was so jubilant that she could have us both. But instead of the response she had expected, my insides were flipping over like a car careening off a mountainside. I took a sip of Amaretto and let some time pass before speaking. Slowly, I said, *"He agreed to let you see me?"* I was upset and sad at the same time. My poor baby was under the illusion that this was what I wanted, too—his *permission* for us to see one another.

I hated to disappoint her, but I had been there before, trying to have an intimate relationship with more than one person at the same time. Those "arrangements" didn't turn out well and it certainly was not going to work for me this time, with her. I did not want Steven to be a part of my relationship with Beth, especially since he would be the one holding all the cards, determining when Beth could and could not see me.

I said, "That's not going to work for me. I'm sorry. I've been there before, and I don't want that now. I don't need or want his permission." My throat clenched up as I spoke. "I think it would be best for us to not see each other anymore. You need to figure things out with Steven."

The blood drained from her face and she looked shrunken, as if someone had sucked the air out of her. Shaking her head in disbelief, Beth said, "No! Please don't do this. I thought you would be happy. I thought we could make it work."

"No, arrangements like these are a fantasy. They don't go well. I saw Howie and Ellen try an open marriage. It didn't work. I wanted an open relationship with Michelle. It failed. I saw other friends try to love more than one person at a time and all those relationships imploded."

"But I'm not them. I don't want to hurt you. I love you so much. Please, honey, please. It will work out. We'll make it work."

My heart was breaking but I had already made my decision. I just shook my head no.

Beth continued, "We can work anything out. Please don't do this."

"I have to. I love you but I can't be in a relationship with you *and* Steven. I'm sorry."

I couldn't believe that I was pulling away from her yet again. It felt like I was traveling through a time warp and it was 1966 at Buffalo State once more, when I retreated from her because it was no longer healthy for me to be around her.

After a few more moments of silence, she looked up at me despondently, nodded, and then walked out.

•

Every day after that I longed for her. I was devastated and walked around in a daze. I felt disabled, like a heart amputee. At the club, I was utterly depressed and it showed. After several weeks, it became too much to bear and my resolve broke down.

That night at my apartment, the phone rang, and it was Dotty. We talked for a few minutes, but I could sense that Beth was there beside her.

"Is Beth there with you?" I asked.

"Yes," Dotty answered.

"Can I speak to her?" I asked.

After a moment, Dotty said, "Hold on."

Beth's voice quavered. "Hello?"

Frightened she would reject me, I barely got out the words. "Will you come over? I need to talk to you." I had devised a strategy that I thought would allow me to make a go of it with her, at least for a while. I had to do something. I couldn't be without her.

"Yes. Give me a few minutes. I'll be right there."

Minutes later Beth stood outside my door, filled with apprehension, like a lost child. We embraced and held each other so closely we could feel each other's heartbeat.

"I missed you so much," I said.

Her voice still quavering, she said, "I missed you, too."

We settled on the couch. I had carefully thought out how I could manage to see her while she was still with Steven. I began speaking as she listened attentively. "I've thought about this a lot. I don't want to be without you. I can't give you up entirely. I can still see you while you're with Steven but with some conditions that I need you to agree to."

She said, "Okay, tell me."

"Okay. This is what I need. One, please do *not* tell Steven you're seeing me. Let him think it's over. I don't want him to be involved in our relationship. This has to be between you and me, only."

Beth nodded and continued to listen.

"And two," I said, "Please don't make me any promises about the future. I don't want to *hope* for anything. I just want to try and live and enjoy each moment with you when we're together. If there are no expectations of a future, there will be less disappointment. Do you understand? Can you do that?"

Although I knew she dreaded deceiving Steven, she said, "Yes. I'll do whatever you want. I don't want to lose you again."

•

On the nights that I worked at Sahara, I'd climb into bed at 6:00 A.M. after a long night, only to be awakened at 7:00 A.M. by Beth's phone call. "Steven's left to go upstate," she'd say into the phone. "I'm coming over."

I'd anxiously await her, eager as a teenager. I'd unlock the front door so she could let herself in and then I'd try to fall back asleep. Of course, I made sure to position myself so that I would be enticing to her when she opened the door and saw me: one arm behind my head like a reclining odalisque, my naked body covered by the blanket in just the right places. When Beth arrived, she'd quietly enter the room and climb into bed next to me. She'd gently wrap herself around me and we would fall back to sleep in each other's arms.

When we awoke, we hung out in my living room for hours on end, talking about our lives, drinking Amaretto, and listening to Stevie Wonder's *Songs in the Key of Life*, an album we especially loved. She often pulled me up from the couch to dance and hold me to her, every part of her body pressed against mine, so that we could feel the blood running through each other's veins. She would softly sing in my ear "Knocks Me off My Feet." Music again deeply connected us as it had in the past.

For the narrow window of time we had together, before Steven returned from his trips, my living room transformed into a magical kingdom of suspended, shimmering air particles, swollen minutes of time, and utter bliss. I can only imagine that it was like the sensation of those spiritual few who have experienced ascending into the light.

We were lost in each other, until we were forced by the repulsive ticking of the clock to disrupt our spell and pay attention to the real world. Ticktock, ticktock. Each minute that passed meant that Steven was one minute closer to returning home, when she would have to leave. We dreaded it. The passing hours became our worst enemy. To remind me of her when she wasn't there, Beth left rose petals and pearls in a glass vase that sat on my windowsill so I would remember her presence.

.

Whether it was just a matter of time before she left Steven or not, I couldn't say for sure, but I inherently trusted her. The intensity of Beth's love, her passionate letters, and her daring recklessness, showed that she was serious and ready to risk everything. The fact that Sahara had grown exponentially in popularity, meaning I was very busy, proved to be the perfect distraction for me during this unsettling time.

When Steven was out of town, Beth occasionally came to the club with me at night, which was very much against her nature. The initial sensory onslaught of entering the packed room was exhilarating for me, but for Beth it could be torturous. She suffered from social anxiety, a disorder that, at that time, had no name. Looking back, I now know it's what plagued her in college, too. While I was transported by the energy of the crowd, riding the waves of people's excitement like a surfer on a grand swell, for her, that much energy could manifest in severe sensory overload. The sounds and energy of too many people filling a room, the strong scents, flashing lights, and deafening sound system, created in her the state of fight or flight, a physiological reaction that occurred in response to her perceived harm. I felt her body stiffen and saw her eyes open wide and her pupils dilate from fear. Walking through the packed lounge and up to the dance floor, she would proceed slowly, carefully, like she was entering a minefield where a wrong step could cost her a limb. I instinctively pulled her close to me so she would feel protected and safe, our bodies tightly interlocked as if we were each other's prized possessions, as we maneuvered through the crowd. I could hear the comments as the women noticed Beth for the first time.

"Who's that with Leslie?"

"Don't know, never saw her before. She's gorgeous . . ."

"Wow, look at Leslie. She's so into her."

•

For months, stealing time, dreading the moment she would have to leave me, and hiding our love from Steven became our full-time preoccupations. It just got harder and harder. I understood what she was going through—wanting something that she didn't know how to have. She had been born into the world in an accepted way, as a heterosexual female, a way in which I had not. She had lived a certain life, and to change it all seemed a Herculean feat. I didn't want to love a straight woman. I was frightened. It could destroy me again, as it did when I fell in love with Suri.

I stayed silent about our dilemma, not wanting to influence her decision in any way, and Beth continued to communicate what she was feeling whenever she was overcome by fear. She wrote:

Les,
You know I'm all talked out . . . I've realized that my fears have taken over. My fears are smothering my being from breathing, blocking my soul. I'm closing the door on my instincts—of being, growing, exploding.

That's because I'm talking myself out of my life. I'm fucking up. I'm not "being." I'm chopping my energy, splicing my essence—trying to fit into some word in the dictionary—label it, classify it, categorize it—dissecting my feelings under a microscope like some kind of fucking amoeba.

I just want to break out and let myself go. The trip is that at times with you, I feel that I'm going, moving, being. It's all sensation—just being—no thinking.

The unexplainable between us is, I see now, exactly THAT. It can't be explained. IT JUST IS.

I'm going to fuck up over and over again—punish myself from time to time—but I'm aware and right now for this very moment I'm dynamite.

I'm living and experiencing you . . . me . . . us.

January 5, 1977, tormented by her indecision, she wrote:

What the hell is going on? I say to you, "I love you. I miss you." And then I say to myself, "Hey Beth, you are saying this to a woman." Then, I ask myself: "Does it make a difference?" Then I say: "I don't know." Do I want it to work with Steven? Do I want it to work with you? Am I being honest? Am I being defensive?

I know that some texture of our relationship is totally unexplainable and that baffles me. What is it, baby? Feeling you in my arms for hours and hours . . . you stroking me with such tenderness it makes me cry. All of my pain, hurt, and disillusionment break down under your touch as I melt into you. I am protected and sheltered by you. The way my beauty is reflected in your eyes embarrasses me. What do I do with you? I want it answered but I know I haven't connected with it yet.

What would my life be like if I were to share it with you? Is it feasible? Do we resist the intimacy between us? Do we love it for the time being? You are on my mind. You appear in my images, flashes of our embraces. I always want to have you.

May our relationship put soft lines on your face and not weariness in your soul.

·

The next month, Beth finally found an apartment on East 87th Street for her and Steven. As often as possible, I would pick her up from work at Dotty's garment center showroom and drive her back home to Steven and their new apartment, in order to spend whatever precious moments I could with her in my car. We'd park down the street so we would not be detected, until she had to leave.

Frustrations grew. The confusion, deception, and hiding became too much to bear. One night in my apartment, her emotional dam finally broke. She suddenly attacked me and aggressively wrestled me to the floor in my bedroom and, while rolling around, struggled hard to pin me down. I fought back. Her softness had somehow disappeared. Her hands, fueled by her exasperation, were stronger than I imagined. Panting and groans spilled from both of us as we competed for control. Her legs flailed in the air. Finally, I was able to hold her down on the floor, my hands keeping her hands tucked close to her body. Then when I felt her body surrender and loosen, I let her go. We lay exhausted and satiated, on our backs on the bedroom floor, and started to laugh uncontrollably.

Despite the emotional troubles that plagued us, despite her uncertainty, Beth was as straightforward and candid as she could be. I was perfectly aware that choosing me would result in a tremendous paradigm shift for a woman who had always been into men.

At times, I was so filled with apprehension from not knowing what my future held that I didn't know if I could bear it much longer. I would not try to force a decision. It had to come from her. One night, after she left me at the club, I wrote her a letter that I never sent, because to do so would have been counterproductive.

Beth,

You left me tonight at the club at midnight to go home to Steven. Understandably, he was hurting, and you love him, and I love you, and you love me, and . . .

"Ring around the rosy . . .

All fall down."

I went down to the office to be alone and, like a spot bouncing off circles on a radar screen, recoiled off the feelings caused by your absence. I want to share them with you. I'm in love with you. I am part of you and you of me. I am your Siamese twin after the bodies have been separated. We are timeless. You were my love before I was in my mother's womb. I adore your smile and your laugh, with its tinge of madness. You know when I cry for the father I never had by the look in my eyes.

And baby, you are so damn beautiful. I lust for you, wanting every inch of you pressed up against me, passing our heat back and forth, until we're depleted.

I'm frightened by this whole thing. It's not so much the intensity of my feelings because that goes on regardless. I accept it and want to ride with it. What frightens me is that I've been down this road before and it didn't work; the ambivalence, the disappointment . . .

You are being pulled in opposite directions. I understand. It's terribly difficult to ride the fence. Eventually decisions have to be made. Lives are changed and people get hurt.

I am a gay woman. I own a predominately gay bar. I fully accept loving another woman. I prefer it. You're a newborn in this world. It could take years for you to totally accept loving me and then again it may not happen at all. Or worse, you may love me with one eye open and with your other eye, look for the "right" guy. I'll know this and it will be torture.

I know you need time. You're not ready to make any decisions. This is my side that's all. I'm impatient and frustrated by limitations. I don't like waiting, hoping. I want you to come from a place of certainty. Our experience together is always cut short. It's unnatural, as if we're both dancing to a record, absorbed in each other, and someone keeps knocking the arm off the turntable. The piercing scratch of the needle skidding across the record is acutely unnerving. That's what happens when you chop our love off, not because you do not want to be with me, but out of your desire to protect what you have with Steven. I can't go backwards and to continue to accept this is going backwards.

It's your life. Who do you want to spend it with? Please take a long hard look at what we have and what I mean to you. I'm choosing to be frustrated for the moment, rather than give you up but I'll be very disappointed with myself if I hang around for too long in a situation where the expansiveness of my love is hampered or not returned in kind. It's ironic. You showed me that I could love intensely again. You helped me realize that I want nothing less.

I had to give myself a time limit. I could not wait indefinitely for Beth to make up her mind. I would hang on another six months. No more, no less.

•

With each week that passed, Beth moved further and further away from Steven, emotionally and psychologically. She began to long for us to stay at her apartment instead of mine. Beth was highly sensitive to the beauty of her surroundings. That she would prefer her apartment to mine was understandable. My apartment was a railroad flat. You entered directly into the tiny bedroom that held my platform bed, the only piece of furniture on the dark purple carpeting, a leftover from the previous tenant. It had two windows that faced a brick wall about three feet away, so the room was dark and airless. An unread pile of the *New York Times* sat by the side of the bed. Loose change was scattered around the floor and sometimes found its way into the unmade bed. Beth did the best she could to clean things up, but the style of the room was beyond salvaging. Although I greatly appreciated beauty, I had little bent for creating it myself.

When Beth knew Steven was going to be away for a few days, she would plead with me, "He's gone. Why don't you stay with me tonight?"

I tried to reject her invitation. "No, I don't think so. I don't think it would be right."

She insisted. "Please. I need to feel your presence there . . . I want you to be with me in *my* bed . . . I want to smell you on *my* sheets."

After she tried several more times to convince me, I succumbed. When I finally entered her apartment, the scent surrounded me like I was being submerged in a bouquet of roses. I descended two stairs into her sunken living room decorated with French country furniture. Behind that was her small bedroom, which opened out to a ground-floor garden. The aroma of rose water engulfed her bed linens, seducing me from across the room. Beth was fastidious about things like clean sheets and perfectly made beds (with a cover sheet, no less). Her apartment was spotless, fresh, and sprinkled with baskets full of flowers and lovely objets d'art—candlesticks, bowls filled with patchouli, and colored-glass vases—arranged like a still life painting.

•

We lay in her bed after making love, the door to the garden open, being caressed by the air, smoking cigarettes, reveling in our love. Oh, if she would only stay in my arms, forever, I thought.

The night after that first visit to her home on February 23, 1977, she wrote me:

> God, I want you here so much more than one night. I want
> to try it alongside you for a while to allow the relationship to
> blossom. I'm so truly sorry that my conditions grate against the
> progression of love. I'm selfish. I wanted your essence left on my
> surroundings—your smell, your touch, your life meshed into
> mine. . . . There's never enough time . . .

On March 30, 1977, over five months since Adrienne's birth-day party, she wrote this note while lying in her bed:

Les, I'm lying in the candlelight
dancing to the music of the wind—
door open
air caresses
smelling
remembering
sighing.
What will happen?
Only time knows.
Introducing you to my family
my life.
Wow! What will happen?
A roller coaster ride baby
climbing ever so slowing, stretching
once over the climb . . .
BethLeslie

12

Virginia Slims

Even though I was off on Thursday nights, I felt obligated to be at Sahara to oversee the acts I booked. I often went to the club on Friday and Saturday nights, too, because those were our busiest nights and I needed to be there to help. Besides, I was extremely proud of what we had accomplished and wanted to share in our success with Michelle, Barbara, and Linda. So, I worked the club during the day and cocktail hours all week, and spent the busiest nights there as well.

Regulars were accustomed to flirting with me. Former lovers overtly pressed their bodies against mine in that familiar way they had done so many times before. However, when Beth began to accompany me to Sahara, my previous flirtatious demeanor totally changed. I was no longer available. Now, I would look apologetically over at Beth, this mysterious woman standing next to me who nobody had ever seen before, and awkwardly pull away from them. Eventually, they got the message—the "up-for-anything Leslie" no longer existed and was now with someone who was clearly off-limits. There was no more sharing of lovers, no more one from Group A and one from Group B, no more casual pickups on the subway or elsewhere. It became obvious that I had fallen in love and that the rules had drastically changed.

At the end of the night, while the staff and owners went downstairs to the office to count the money and check out their registers, Beth waited upstairs in the lounge. She usually fell asleep on one of the couches, covered by my Guatemalan wool cape. After everyone left, I would join her on the couch, lying down next to her until she stirred.

We would continue to lie in each other's arms, just the two of us in the empty space. All the lights were out in the club. Floating dust particles, lit only by the jukebox lights and the white fluorescent lights from under the bar, filled the room and lingered in front of our eyes. The only sounds, other than the music from the jukebox, were the clunking of newly made ice cubes dropping into the ice machine and the buzz from the fluorescent lights. The haunting sound of Boz Scaggs's "Harbor Lights" streamed through the air.

As the sun rose over the Manhattan skyline, we would reluctantly lift ourselves off the couch to venture into the emerging dawn. Sunlight stabbed at our still adjusting eyes. We held each other close to shelter ourselves from the real world—city growls and the masses scurrying past us on their way to work—and made our way home.

•

Upon Steven's return from Woodstock, he held my pack of Virginia Slims in his hand and shook it in front of Beth's face. It had accidently fallen behind the bed when I had stayed at their apartment, and Steven had discovered them.

"What is this?" he said to her.

"Oh my God!" I said to Beth, later, as she tried to reenact what happened.

She said to me, "Baby, I told him everything. I told him that I had been seeing you all along. I told him . . . I said . . . 'I'm in love with Leslie. It's over between us. I'm so sorry.'"

"What did he do?" I asked, shaken by the news.

"He screamed at me and threw things around the apartment . . . and then he cried." Tears fell from her eyes as she said, "And I cried, too. Les, he was always a kind and gentle man. I hate the pain I'm causing him, but it was inevitable." As she spoke, Beth was reliving the wrenching scene in her mind. Her face reddened, and she cried even harder. I took her in my arms.

"I'm so sorry," I said.

Beth's voice wavered with emotion. "It was just a matter of time."

I could tell that she had no regrets, but she was aware of the gravity of her decision. "How do you feel now?" I asked.

"I feel free." Wiping her tears, she said, "Les, I'm finally yours."

Now, finally, we were together—without limitations or constraints. She was mine and I was hers. The irony of all this was that, when Beth finally decided to choose me, she not only made the radical change of sharing her life with a woman instead of a man but with someone, no less, who had become a "star" in the lesbian world. As Sahara's notoriety grew, so did my personal profile and that of my partners. Because of my job, in order for us to spend time together, Beth was forced to become immersed in the lesbian club scene. Not even lesbians have to do that!

•

Beth's next move was to write a letter to her mother. She chose May 3, 1977, to give it to her as a Mother's Day gift, because she naively thought this news would bring her mother joy. *Oy*. She gave me a copy of the letter, which I saved.

May 3, 1977

Dear Mom,

The most beautiful aspect of living is owning one's life. Doing what feels right—taking responsibility. We are individuals with different perceptions, needs and attitudes. To be a healthy person, is to be connected with these needs and perceptions, and hopefully be fulfilled.

We are in this game for ourselves. If not, fulfillment and satisfaction will never come our way. I am not living my life for anybody or according to society's dictates.

TO EACH HIS OWN . . .

My life is Beth Suskin and Leslie Cohen. I have finally met my match. I have fallen in love with a person who understands and adores me. It is quite an INCREDIBLE relationship. All my needs are fulfilled. There is no doubt that we are spiritually connected and have always been, even back more than twelve years ago when we first met in Buffalo.

Les is real, alive, happy, intelligent, loving, sensual, artistic, and sensitive and loved by many. Her soul is my soul—music to the nth degree, art, theater, nature—colors in our environment—everything. Her enthusiasm is my enthusiasm. There is never enough time. When we are walking through the streets, walking into stores, eating in restaurants, the constant remark is: "You two look so happy." We are. I am.

According to society, it's unfortunate that she is a woman. But for my life, it's the most fortunate thing that's happened to me. I must do what is best for Beth. Les appreciates me and respects me the way no one ever has. It's like being a young girl and having a sleepover date, whispering under the covers with your best friend.

I respect her enormously and am proud to be part of her life. I could not, in my right mind, leave her and be with Steven. Steven satisfies many needs of mine—I still love him—but I was never totally satisfied. Steven fulfilled me emotionally and sexually, but not intellectually and did not fulfill my sensual nature. Steven helped me greatly but not in the present. I am not growing, experiencing with him. Les feeds me in every way. Do I give this fantastic relationship up? How can I?

Steven knows what has happened. We are working it out. When his auction plans are definite, he will be moving. I'm going to keep the apartment.

Everything will work out because I want it to.

As I expected, when her mother received the letter, it didn't go over well. Actually, it was a disaster. Beth said, "My mom freaked out! 'Leslie Cohen? What do you mean Leslie Cohen? Leslie Cohen's a woman! You were always boy crazy. This is totally out of left field. Are you trying to hurt me? I don't understand what you're talking about!'"

And then Beth looked at me and said, "It doesn't matter. She doesn't get it. She may never get it. I finally have the wisdom to know what's right and wrong for me. If my mother only knew how I was ripping myself into shreds and hating myself, how I was in conflict all the time and so sad."

My heart swelled with empathy for her. "I'm so sorry."

She continued, "My darling, I always knew I was going to have to fight for my life. But I also knew I was going to find somebody in my life who loved me the way I wanted to be loved. Les, you were my opportunity. You enabled me to heal. You, the love of my life, gave me my life back. My sweet baby, you did that for me."

•

Beth loved me in a way no one else ever had, other than my mother. She even loved my pudgy hands, which were clearly neither definitively male nor female in appearance. Beth found my hands to be outrageous and delightful and described them in a way that only she could. My short fingernails and the skin surrounding them reminded her of the old headgear that deep-sea divers used to wear. The shape of my fingers, the thickness around the knuckles that then tapered to a flattened, narrowed tip, resembled gherkin pickles to her. The way my hands spread out when trying to demonstrate a point, she described as starfish moving along the ocean floor. She compared their scent to sugar wafers. My hands represented my male-female duality that she found so appealing.

And I loved her hands, which, once again, were so incongruous with the rest of her. They were farmer's hands and not particularly feminine or pretty. They moved as a solid mass, more clumsy than graceful. Her fingers and wrists lacked flexibility, like dog's paws rather than human hands, and her arms were extremely long. The vision of her long arms and those "clumps" (my comical name for them) hanging at the end of them like weights tickled me no end. We loved each other for what made us unique, and we knew, in a profound way, that this was a very unusual and precious gift that we gave each other.

•

It took another ten months after Beth left Steven for me to put my possessions in storage and move into her apartment. Initially, I fought it. I thought she needed time to clear away the cobwebs of her life with Steven, time to be by herself. I was also scared that she didn't fully realize how difficult I could be and what she was getting herself into living with me.

Living out of a suitcase, running from my place to Beth's apartment and then to our summer time-share on Fire Island, which we rented for our first summer together, was becoming unmanageable. But I wanted to adequately prepare her so she could change her mind about living together, if need be.

I sat her down one evening before the move, after she had cooked us a delicious meal. There was still half a bottle of wine left and I suggested we share it.

"Sweetheart, I need to talk to you," I started.

"What is it?" She said.

"I just want to warn you about me. There are some things you should know."

"I know everything I need to know. What don't I know about you?"

"Well," I started slowly. "I'm difficult, moody, and sometimes downright melancholic. There are times I need to be alone to balance myself out."

"That's fine. I don't care," she said.

"I might want to sleep by myself on the living room couch, just to regroup."

"No problem," she said. "You do whatever you need to do." (It never happened.)

"One last thing," I said. "You know I'm a slob and I know that beautiful surroundings are important to you."

"That's true. So, let's make a deal. How about you make the bed, wash the dishes, and clean the ashtrays?" We both smoked at the time. "That's all you have to do. I'll do everything else."

Surprised at how simple she made it, I said, "Yes, I can do that."

Beth said, "Is there anything else you need to warn me about?"

"No. I think we're done here," I said and kissed her soft lips.

•

Beth was the refuge that I returned to after my nights at the club. Grungy, exhausted, and stinking from booze and cigarettes,

I undressed and climbed into the deftly made bed that she had prepared and felt a wave of purity and cleanliness envelope me, like a baptism. Pressing against her warm skin, I would kiss her neck and inhale her scent as she slept. Gently, I'd lift her nightgown above her waist, trying not to wake her, and rest my head in the small, deep crater of her back, just above her butt, which was covered in a delicate down and held my head perfectly like a cradle.

Then, I would slide a bit farther down her body and softly kiss her bottom, with its skin as untouched and precious as a child's. There, I would rest my head until the mixture of her nakedness and scent calmed me down enough from the adrenaline rush of the night to move back up to my own pillow. With her image fading under my eyelids and her body next to mine, I'd fall asleep.

PART III

A Posse of Outsiders

13
Lone Riders

When the prospect of opening Sahara had been looming on the horizon, I became quite a promoter, constantly talking up my hopes and dreams for the club to whomever would listen. When I met Alix Kucker, a woman who had expertise with concert production and political fundraising, at a party, I said to her, "I'm about to open a nightclub for women with my three partners, and it's going to be extraordinary—very 'out,' on Second Avenue. We want it to be more than merely a bar. We want it to be a gathering place for women—we want political activity, live entertainment, art—we want the whole mix. Would you be able to help?" Seduced by my enthusiasm, she agreed without knowing what she had gotten herself into. Regardless, she became a driving force behind Sahara's success, and I am forever indebted to her.

Elaine Noble was the first openly gay person to run and subsequently be elected to state legislature in the United States; she served in the Massachusetts House of Representatives. A former college professor of Alix's, Elaine had asked Alix to help her raise funds for her campaign and Alix connected her to Sahara. One day Alix called me in the office and said, "How would you like to have Jane Fonda at the club?" I almost fell off my chair. Thus the event for Elaine Noble became Sahara's first fundraising event, occurring on July 8, 1976, only two months after the club opened. Alix and I worked together to do everything we could to make it a hit. Alix,

FIG. 22. Flyer for Elaine Noble fundraiser featuring Jane Fonda and Tom Hayden; Pat Benatar sang but she wasn't yet famous.

through Elaine, had connections to Gloria Steinem, Jane Fonda, and Fonda's then husband Tom Hayden, and they were all among the guests that night. The evening raised a tremendous amount of money as well as everyone's consciousness that Sahara was much more than a traditional women's bar.

The fundraiser also put Sahara on the map with a wider audience of accomplished women. The event was packed. Judy Licht, a reporter for one of the local news programs, even covered it. Alix's

FIG. 23. Jane Fonda, Elaine Noble, and Alix Kucker at Elaine's fundraiser at Sahara.

company, Red One Productions, partnered with Sahara many more times after that, becoming the "official" producer of women's sophisticated political events in New York City.

After Elaine Noble's first event, Alix and I organized another fundraiser for her on January 25, 1977, with Gilda Radner, Laraine Newman, and Jane Curtin, the stars of NBC's very popular *Saturday Night Live*, appearing on her behalf. Gilda did her Baba Wawa (Barbara Walters) character. The infamous skit of Barbara Walters interviewing "Gloria Steinem" (played by Jane Curtin) was hysterical, especially since Gloria Steinem was in the Sahara audience, enjoying it as much as everyone else. Pat Benatar performed. We also had the entire cast of the musical *The Club*, a group of women all dressed as men wearing top hats and tails, tap dancing and singing on our small stage. The show, directed by Tommy Tune and written by Eve Merriam, garnered ten Obies that year—the off-Broadway equivalent of a Tony.

FIG. 24. Flyer for Elaine Noble fundraiser featuring Jane Curtin, Gilda Radner, Gloria Steinem, and Pat Benatar (spelled incorrectly).

The next benefit we threw, on August 23, 1977, was for the unforgettable New York politician Bella Abzug, who was running for mayor of New York City. It featured guest appearances by Gloria Steinem and the actress Louise Lasser. The media called our guest of honor "Battling Bella" due to her relentless and feisty style. She was a lawyer, a member of the U.S. House of Representatives, and one of the pivotal voices in the women's movement. Along with Gloria Steinem, Shirley Chisholm, and Betty Friedan, she cofounded the National Women's Political Caucus, which aimed to increase the participation of women in government. People either loved her or hated her. We loved her.

On September 6, 1977, a benefit for Carol Bellamy, who was running for city council president for New York City, was held at Sahara. Authors Betty Friedan, Gloria Steinem, and Robin Morgan and playwrights Eve Merriam and Ntozake Shange (the latter being known for *For Colored Girls Who Have Considered Suicide / When the Rainbow Is Enuf*) appeared. It was a remarkable night. I acted as the emcee, introducing everyone from the stage, overwhelmed that I was in the presence of such extraordinary women, the pillars of the feminist movement.

I was still in awe of and nervous around all of the celebrities who came to Sahara that night to support Bellamy. To top it off, Patti Smith and Pat Benatar appeared. All eyes were on Patti Smith when she approached the stage to recite one of her inciting, angry, and profanity-laced poems. At one point in the reading, Patti ferociously spat out the forbidden word, "*tits*," as if she were challenging the audience to a duel. As soon as the word hit the air, I felt a shudder come over the room.

The radical feminists in the audience squirmed uncomfortably, as if they had been personally assaulted, and immediately hurled loud boos at the stage. The word *tits*, as used by men, was always particularly offensive because it clearly objectified women. Feminists, understandably, believed that words were the catalysts for bigger things like oppression, and they weren't standing for it.

On the other hand, the younger women in the audience were clearly amused; they encouraged Patti because they loved her fearless bravado. It felt different when the word *tits* came from the mouth of a woman rather than a man. This newer generation had begun to absorb the concepts of feminism, incorporating them into their lives. Whereas the word *tits* could be distasteful to those who had fought so hard, in the past, to not be treated as sexual objects,

FIG. 25. Flyer for Carol Bellamy fundraiser featuring Betty Friedan, Eve Merriam, Robin Morgan, Ntozake Shange, Gloria Steinem, and a surprise appearance by Patti Smith.

it now became a cry of liberation when it was uttered by someone of their own generation. Smith was an outlaw, doing her own thing, saying whatever the hell she pleased. Feminism was evolving and expanding its audience in front of our eyes. Unflinchingly, Patti continued her performance. But for me, in that moment, the intricacies

FIG. 26. Star-studded cast of feminists at Sahara for Bellamy fundraiser: left to right, top to bottom: Betty Friedan, Robin Morgan, Karen Burstein, Gloria Steinem, Eve Merriam, me, Jane Trichter, Ronnie Eldridge, Alix Kucker and Ntozake Shange; these were all special nights to remember as Sahara became a center for political fundraising for female politicians. Photo credit: Nancie Gee.

of the politics of newly empowered women became clear; we were watching it unfold in real time.

Sahara's mere existence helped to assimilate second-wave feminist concepts into the broader lesbian culture. Although I had immense admiration and deep gratitude for the early feminists' struggles on women's behalf, at Sahara we wanted to resist any myopic view of what it meant to be a feminist. As Anselma Dell'Olio wrote in 1970, "Women's [radical feminist] rage, masquerading as a pseudo-egalitarian radicalism under the 'pro-woman' banner," was turning into "frighteningly vicious anti-intellectual fascism of the left."[1] Some of the more radical feminists thought that the women who came to Sahara didn't qualify as "feminist" enough. Sahara was called elitist because of its location in a predominately white upper-middle-class neighborhood. We were not considered intelligent or serious enough in our devotion to the cause because we were "fashionable," which to some of the women in the movement meant frivolous. To me, it didn't make sense to break out of one box just to be put into another. Being a feminist was all about *freedom and choice.*

Instead of using angry rhetoric, we were just prowoman, constantly showing what women were capable of by showcasing their art, music, and politics. Art, poetry, and the intellectual writings of women made such a difference in my own life that I wanted to provide that to other women who dearly needed to see positive role models. Sahara may have started out simply as a sophisticated club for women, but it quickly became a *movement.*

I looked around the room that night and was filled with a deep sense of pride and personal satisfaction. This was what Sahara was about—the confluence of women with varying viewpoints who ultimately all wanted the same thing: equality, freedom, opportunity, and respect. It was history in the making. It was art.

As an interesting historical side note, Betty Friedan, the first president and cofounder of the National Organization of Women (NOW), had tried to exclude lesbians from the feminist movement at a NOW conference in 1969. The phrase "Lavender Menace" was coined by her to describe the threat that she believed associations with lesbianism posed to NOW and the emerging women's movement. Friedan, along with other heterosexual feminists, worried that the inclusion of lesbians would hamstring the ability of the feminist movement to achieve serious political change, and that stereotypes of "mannish" and "man-hating" lesbians would provide an easy way for mainstream society to dismiss the movement. But here she was in September of 1977 at Sahara, a predominantly lesbian club. Interestingly enough, in November 1977, less than two months after her appearance at Sahara, Betty Friedan apologized for her promotion of the exclusion of lesbians as "disrupters" of the women's movement at the National Women's Conference in Houston, and actively supported a resolution against sexual orientation discrimination. I would like to think that her experiences at Sahara played a role in her decision.

Sahara became the birthplace of "lesbian chic" in the United States. Over the next few years, the star power continued at Sahara. Week after week, some of the greatest women artists, writers, poets, singers, and speakers came to share their wisdom on the Sahara stage. This included authors Kate Millett, Rita Mae Brown, Florynce Kennedy, Adrienne Rich, and vocalists Sheila Jordan, Lana Cantrell, Nona Hendryx, and Julie Budd. There were many others, including a lot of the glamorous personalities of the day.

•

After these special events the disco would open and everyone would rush upstairs, drawn by the throbbing of the bass speakers. I remember Bella and Gloria dancing upstairs amongst the hundreds of women to Thelma Houston's "Don't Leave Me This Way." Sahara was the first club to showcase female DJs like Ellen Bogen and Sharon White who became the earliest female resident DJs in the United States. They opened the doors for other women DJs in clubs around New York City, and both went on to become record promoters: Ellen at Casablanca Records, home of Donna Summer, and Sharon White at Motown, home of Marvin Gaye. Sahara was a showcase for the big disco artists of the time—Grace Jones, Linda Clifford, Dr. Buzzard's Original Savannah Band, and Sylvester—who came to visit Sharon and Ellen in the DJ booth at Sahara to promote their records.

The DJs kept the music pumping, and hundreds of people of every size, shape, color, and economic background danced together in unison. The walls would literally sweat from all the people packed into that relatively small space. The end of the evening was the

FIG. 27. Invitation for Sahara's second anniversary featuring Nona Hendryx (spelled incorrectly); this was the box design we used for our monthly advertisements in the *Village Voice*.

hardest. The crowd collectively moaned when they heard what a friend referred to as "the fucking 'Last Dance,'" Donna Summer's legendary anthem, which signaled the end of another night. The party was over. And when they finally arrived home, the schoolteachers, nurses, lawyers, housewives, and businesswomen reluctantly prepared themselves for reentry into their closeted realities. That next day, amidst their varying chores and duties, I always imagined that they couldn't help reminiscing about the night before—*the club, the club, the club.*

•

When I worked both day and night shifts, Beth would meet me at Sahara and we would go to dinner before I had to return to the club, often to a restaurant nearby called Maxwell's Plum. Maxwell's Plum was an opulent rococo creation. With its outlandish art nouveau décor—kaleidoscopic stained glass on the ceilings and walls, Tiffany lamps, a menagerie of ceramic animals, etched glass, and cascades of crystal—the restaurant was the "it" place at the time.

Usually, we would be seated facing each other at a table for two, but within minutes, we would change seats so that we could sit side by side on the banquette with our bodies pressed together, openly demonstrative toward one another. If someone had an issue with that, Beth deemed it their problem, not ours. We were deliriously in love and Beth refused to hide it. It was always amazing to me that Beth could be so indifferent to the judgment that came with being out. She was so grateful for and proud of our love that she believed, in her naïveté, strength, and courage, that what we had was a remarkable gift that others should see and appreciate. She just didn't give a damn what people thought.

Ironically, I felt more uncomfortable than she did being so "out" in public, which only made me recognize that, as visible and brave as I thought I was opening Sahara, the oppression I had unconsciously absorbed over the years had closed me off. When Beth turned to me and kissed me on my lips, it left little doubt in the minds of those around us of the nature of our relationship. Her audacity often embarrassed me, as I awkwardly averted my eyes from the other diners. It was not easy facing out into a crowded restaurant, seeing the curious stares or shared whispers of the other customers. But Beth was so proud of our love that she felt it was our responsibility to educate people—to *show them what two women in love looked like*. I understood and agreed. Visibility was the only way to change minds.

Because we were attractive, Beth and I knew we were good role models. It became our mission to enlighten others. We presented an alluring visual picture to the straight world to combat the negative stereotypes that endured about what being gay meant. I'm sure that alone influenced people, but the fact was, we were so apparently in love that it was infectious to those around us. Quarrelling couples stopped fighting. Cranky and tired restaurant staff became playful. Neighboring tables smiled warmly at us to show their receptiveness. Often, we were bought dessert or drinks on the house, as an acknowledgment for what we literally brought to the table. It was transformative for others to see us and we knew it.

In 1977, it definitely was a bold decision to be out, to reveal to the straight world that there was nothing for them to be afraid of and to the gay world that we were willing to chance it. We understood that it was difficult for straight people to understand or empathize with same-sex couples if they never *saw* them. Invisibility made it easier for others to demonize us. Thus, for us, visibility was the key to awareness and positive change.

Even our gay friends felt uncomfortable when they were with us and we were outwardly affectionate in public. "Do you have to do that?" they would say, aware that other people were staring at us.

"Yes," we would say. "People *need* to see this." They would shake their heads, knowing they could not convince us otherwise.

Facetiously, I once asked Beth, "How does it feel to bring a lesbian out?" Aware of the paradox, she laughed. We refused to allow anyone to sully our joy because of their own misconceptions and homophobia. It was time to step up to the plate. But it was still scary.

•

I often spent whatever free nights I had going to talent showcases at other cabarets to book acts for our Thursday night shows. Beth started coming with me. Being exposed to all these live acts around the city and at Sahara began to awaken her dormant desire to sing, so we bought her a keyboard and she began to tinker.

Beth was overly sensitive to everything around her, as if she was stripped bare in a snowstorm with nothing to protect her. If she felt exposed, you could see the fear in her eyes, like a cornered animal. She thought that no one accepted her for who she was and only felt protected when she was alone with me. In this regard, she wasn't much different than she had been in college, but as opposed to the constriction I felt in college, now I welcomed it. It buffered the intense and frantic social scene I encountered every night at the club. Being alone with her offered me peace and security, a sense of steadfastness.

I adored her for the hodgepodge she was, but my love alone was not enough. Beth desperately needed to find her own way. I wanted her to come out of her shell and flourish—to realize how incredibly special she was. I hoped that her love of and connection with music would help her get in touch with her own talents and give her the self-confidence she sorely needed.

I was at the club one night when she called from our apartment, elated. She told me that she'd been listening to the jazz artist Earl Klugh all night and had been inspired. "Honey, you have to listen to this," she said. On the other end of the phone I could hear her play a series of chords on her keyboard. She'd made up a tune and began to sing. It was simple and melodious. Her vibrato was gorgeous. Those few notes on the other end of that telephone signaled the beginning of what we had been waiting for, her return to singing.

14

Style Gets Used Up

If you get me alone, I can be shy, but if you get me in a room filled with women, I soar. Managing Sahara turned out to be the perfect job for who I was. It was my means for self-actualization. It gave me the ability to love myself and other women and to express my creative self. Sahara nurtured and expanded me.

At Sahara, there were women from all walks of life, a functioning microcosm of what an ideal society could and should be in all its diversity and inclusion—a mix of straight, gay, intellectual, blue-collar, rich, poor, young, old, black, white, Latina, progressive, and conservative women—mashed together in this safe harbor. We were a posse of outsiders morphed into one band of merry revelers. That's what I loved about it—watching all that interaction take place in one relatively small space and experiencing the real bond that existed between us. We had each other, regardless of where we came from—at least for the night.

Since most of us were lesbians, we were, in certain profound ways, absent from the mainstream of society, perhaps replacing that visibility with an edge of madness and abandon, anonymity fueling even wilder and bolder behavior. For the most part without husbands and most without children, we enjoyed fewer of the burdens and responsibilities of adulthood. At Sahara we were free, sharing a commonality in our gender, sexuality, and the desire to escape from the world's judgments, chaos, and uncertainties through the joys of sex, drugs, and dancing.

The environment at Sahara nourished the aspiration and hope that we could openly be who we were—this hodgepodge of women, this intriguing mix of people and principles with all their wacky incongruities. It's been said that to share happiness is the very noblest thing human beings can aspire to and that is what we did. If only Sahara could have lasted forever! That's like saying if only the world could stop spinning. But, of course, Sahara could not last forever and, over time, joy morphed into pain.

•

My mentor and friend, Dr. Robert Pincus-Witten, once said to me, "Style gets used up." He was referring to art and fashion, but it was also painfully true in the fickle nightclub business. Style was then, and will always be, about *the next new thing*. That phrase articulated the hard truth that I had to face. There was a shelf life for Sahara, and it was running out, not only for the club but for my relationship to it. The absolute euphoria that I experienced at Sahara for the first few years of its existence was life altering, as would be the hell that I experienced toward and after its end.

In the first half of Sahara's existence I felt productive and fulfilled in ways I never had before. However, as the years progressed, the excitement of owning and working in the club clearly ebbed, especially in the last year. The club business is odd. It will give you the greatest life you ever had, but if you are not careful it will take more than you give it. Drugs were often the culprit, at least partially, for their downfalls. My partners were high a lot of the time, and their drug abuse was a problem that eventually interfered with their work. Not to excuse their drug abuse, but I did not have to stay up nights in a row to the wee hours of the morning like them, which I believe was a contributing factor. I was on a different schedule. I tried to reason with them, but I could not change their behavior. My feelings of helplessness, purposelessness, and despair grew. One night, when I realized one of the pieces of art that I had so carefully hung in the hallway stairwell leading to the disco had been damaged by sweat, I totally wigged out, spewing my frustrations. Afterward, I wrote in my diary:

Once upon a time, there was a young woman who owned a nightclub, and surrounded by incompetence and lies, smashed the bar glasses against the walls, shattering them, as everyone who worked there ran for cover, hiding under cocktail tables and behind the bar. The walls in the disco had sweated the night before from body heat, dripping moisture down on and staining her precious artwork hanging in the stairwell. The next day, Chen, the porter, tried to wash the stains off, not realizing that the art was "art," only damaging it further.

When she saw what happened, she went berserk because art was all she had left that was pure and meaningful to her. She screamed and began kicking in the metal lockers in the basement. With each crashing sound of her shoe against metal, echoing off the cement walls, floors and gurgling pipes, BANG, BANG, BANG, she raged.

Her partners continued to work behind their desks in the nearby office, slurring their words while doing business with the iceman, stoned on Quaaludes and coke. Finally, exhausted, she went into the office and collapsed on the bare wooden bench. One of her partners approached, scared straight for a few lucid moments by the clamorous noise, and tentatively asked if she was all right. She nodded yes through her closed eyes.

·

My frustration and anger had been mounting for many months and finally exploded. We, the four partners had grown apart. We were working different shifts and spent little time together outside of work. We no longer shared the intimacy that bonded us when we started Sahara.

When their drug use spiraled out of control I could barely decipher their chicken-scratch notes from the night before, which meandered off the lined page as if they had lost their way. I loved them and worried a lot, for them and for me. Not that I was an angel by any means, but I never allowed drugs to interfere with my work. I had accomplished what I wanted to do with Sahara and was becoming more discontented with each passing day. It got to the point where I saw no solution and just wanted to get the fuck out.

•

Gradually, almost imperceptibly, I had crossed over from my previous life in the art world, with its highbrow aspirations, to the more hedonistic club life. I never became hooked on drugs, like so many in the club business did, but I did become addicted to the adrenaline rush—the exhilaration that I received from the flashing lights, the loud rhythmic sounds of the music, the crowds, the clinking glasses, the constant din of chatter and laughter, the human drama, the sexiness, the touching, the eyes looking at me through the crowd, and the celebrity status I held in the lesbian scene.

I had become a slave to my own needs, as well as the needs of others. For nearly four years, I smiled at and kissed so many people who wanted my attention because I adored the women who came to the club, and I wanted to give something of myself to every one of them. I felt terrible if someone felt ignored or left out. This performance had become a tightrope walk. At times, it was pure ecstasy, surrendering myself entirely to our shared experience. At other times, I was just exhausted. The euphoric feeling was dangerous because if I allowed my ego to take over, if I bought into the myth of my own self-importance, it could easily overcome my substance and authenticity.

One may logically know that it is smarter to pursue anonymity, to try to disappear because life feels more balanced and less dependent that way, but I was not able to do that, not only because I made my living in the nightclub business but also because I didn't want to. My conflict, the drama of which would be played out for years to come, was being formulated—my need to influence people and groups and my desire for fame through recognition versus the awareness of the danger of fame and ego. Without the club, I was afraid I would feel erased, and the nothingness of that choice ached like failure rather than centeredness and independence.

•

While still at Sahara, looking for a way out, I had already started to dabble in exploring other ways to make a living. I started writing a screenplay, briefly studied filmmaking at New York University, and even worked as a production assistant on a few notable films like *Kramer vs. Kramer* and *Wolfen*.

I also explored politics. In 1978 I was appointed to Community Board 8, which represented the Upper East Side of Manhattan and, along with other gay and lesbian activists throughout the city, formed the Lesbians' and Gay Men's Caucus.[1] Our goal was to pass a resolution in support of New York City gay rights legislation[2] that would protect gay citizens against discrimination in the areas of housing, employment, and public accommodations. It was our answer to the antihomosexual campaigns going on at the time in Eugene, Oregon, and Dade County, Florida, the latter led by Anita Bryant.[3] (The "homosexual rights" bill was finally passed on March 20, 1986.)

I was very proud the night we presented our approved resolutions to the city council. We accomplished something very meaningful. But I realized politics was not for me. During long, onerous political discussions, I felt as if I were being "confined to a stuffy meeting room when [I] might have been out [instead] picking violets," to quote Gabriele D'Annunzio.[4] Many kudos and much appreciation to the activists and politicians who can do the tedious legislative work necessary to effect change but I just did not have the patience.

Toward the end of 1979, I talked to Michelle about asking Barbara and Linda to buy us out. If they were taken aback, they didn't show it. They said they were open to the idea and would consider it, but in the meantime, Linda's mother became gravely ill. Barbara and Linda needed Michelle and me to cover their shifts for them at the club while they took care of her. Any further discussion about a buyout was delayed, and then, for reasons which will soon become apparent, never took place.

•

Beth had finally decided to try her hand at singing again and needed to put an act together. She wanted to learn how to bartend so she'd no longer be tied to a nine-to-five job and could work on her new career. On the afternoon of December 26, 1979, she came with me to open the club and begin her bartender training.

When we arrived, I put my key in the door, like I had done every day for almost four years. Strangely, the key did not fit. Unsuccessfully, I tried again and again to jiggle open the lock. It would not budge. I didn't understand. My fear intensified exponentially, as I went from confused to desperate and then angry. I peered through the small window in the front door and saw nothing but darkness. I frantically screamed out, "WHAT THE HELL IS GOING ON HERE?"

I started pounding on the door with my fists, then kicking it and shouting, "LET ME IN! LET ME IN!" Finally, appearing like an apparition out of the darkness was a man with a gun in his hand, who approached the door and waved me away.

"Who the fuck is that?" I said. I screamed at him through the door, "I OWN THIS CLUB! LET ME IN!"

The spook looked at me, shook his head, and said, "Sorry, you'll have to speak to your landlord." I could barely hear him through the door. After several more minutes of trying to get through to the guy, we gave up and went upstairs to Kay's apartment to call Michelle, Barbara, and Linda and explain what happened.

By the time my partners arrived at Kay's apartment, everyone was in a panic. Trying to comprehend the harsh reality of the horror that was taking place, we were in shock, staring at each other, gutted by the potential magnitude of the loss. In a kind of cerebral quicksand, none of us were able to fully process how to respond. Everything we owned—all of our money, inventory, equipment, the DJs' records, and artwork that I either personally owned or was on loan—was padlocked inside that club. Suddenly and without warning, all of our livelihoods had been taken hostage.

Immediately, we called our lawyer, Richard Runes. He had been an associate at Sid Davidoff's firm when we initially put the firm on retainer, and Sid assigned Richard to watch over us. Richard became a regular at the club. A young, highly ambitious lawyer—amiable, paunchy, frizzy haired, and dressed in three-piece suits—he especially befriended Barbara and Linda and often hung out with them socially, either at the club, seduced by the drugs, booze, and women, or at their apartment.

When he got on the phone, we frantically described what had happened, telling him about the guy waving the gun at me and not letting us into the club. He said, "I'll do what I can and get back to you," and hung up, but he never called back. As the hours passed, we became more and more desperate and, at the same time, started getting suspicious about Richard's involvement with Mark Perlbinder, a wealthy real estate developer.

Things had been strange for us ever since Perlbinder bought our building and became our new landlord just a few months earlier. It unfolded like this. One day, before Perlbinder entered the picture, a representative of our then landlord, a bank, who customarily came to the club every month to collect the rent, suggested that we buy the building that housed Sahara. He said the bank did not really want to be in the real estate business and would be eager to accommodate us by selling it to us at a very reasonable price. Because we were so inexperienced with these kinds of transactions, we asked Richard to advise us.

Soon after that, the bank representative told us that Richard had actually brokered the sale of the building to Mark Perlbinder. Of course, Runes never told us about his role in the transaction. It must have been a huge professional score for him to get Perlbinder, a highly successful developer, as a client, even though it was a clear conflict of interest to be representing both of us. Almost immediately, Perlbinder stopped accepting our rent checks, sending them back to us. We didn't understand why and could not get an answer. This went on for three months. During that time, we placed our rent in an escrow account as proof of our attempted payments.

Since we didn't hear back from Runes that night, Barbara called her cousin Anthony, an attorney, to help us. Fortunately, he agreed to immediately file a pro bono lawsuit on our behalf. All that was left to do was call the staff and make up an excuse for them to not come to work that Wednesday night.

On Thursday, December 27, Anthony, whose law office was in Garden City, Long Island, connected with another attorney closer to Manhattan, who quickly filed papers with the court charging that our new landlord, Mark Perlbinder, illegally evicted us by not giving us notice. We rushed to Long Island City to get a copy of the motion and were back in Manhattan by 3:00 P.M., where we served the city marshal's office and Perlbinder's lawyers, hoping that we could reopen in time for the Thursday night show.

But, no matter how many calls we made, no one could locate the city marshal, who had to personally reopen the club for us. The hours ticked by and the city marshal did not return our calls. At 7:00 P.M., we finally heard back from her, only to have her tell us that it was after work hours and too late for her to do anything. We begged and pleaded, but she refused. We found out later that she was a personal friend of Perlbinder's.

We rushed to our local precinct in an attempt to get the police to let us in the building, but they said they needed a court order. A temporary order had been procured but it was at Anthony's office, a forty-five-minute drive away, and there were neither computers nor faxes back then. It was now 8:00 P.M. and the Sahara staff had started to gather outside the club. While Barbara and Linda rushed to Garden City to get a copy of the order, Michelle and I dealt with the staff. The entertainment for the night, Brenda and the Realtones, arrived and waited with us curbside, their instruments and equipment piled high on the sidewalk.

When Linda, Barbara and the police finally arrived at the club, the police realized that they'd have to break into the club because the locks had been changed, which they refused to do until daylight the next day. We desperately begged the officers, their superiors, and anyone else who would listen, but to no avail. A large crowd of customers, along with the staff and band members, were now gathered, waiting to get in, so we told everyone there was an electrical problem in the club and we couldn't open. Finally, everyone dispersed and I dragged myself home, utterly deflated, to Beth.

On Friday, December 28, we went back to the precinct. A high-ranking community affairs officer, Michael, had received a phone call from some gay activists on our behalf who had an ongoing relationship with him and he agreed to help us. After arriving at the club and confronting the armed guard who once again refused to let us in, Michael smashed open the large front window that faced directly onto Second Avenue. Stunned, we stood there and watched the glass shatter and fall to the sidewalk, followed by cascading layers of colored sand and uprooted cacti. All that remained in the window was Sahara's large, iconic wooden logo that had rested on top of the sand and now lay on its side, like an artifact from a bombed-out building.

Michael climbed through the window and opened the front door to let us in. He kept the armed guard at bay. Anthony had told us to grab whatever we could, as fast as we could, because he knew Perlbinder and Runes would be working on getting our court order overturned. We charged into the club like the cavalry, running straight through the lounge, down the stairs, and into the liquor closet in our office to where our cash deposits were held. They were kept in a bag stuffed in a secret hole in the wall behind the liquor bottles.

When we reached into the hole, the bag wasn't there. In fact, nothing was there. *Everything* was gone—our money, all the liquor, and our ledgers. In disbelief, we stared at the bare shelves, once loaded with bottles of Johnnie Walker Black, Stolichnaya, and Courvoisier. There was now no doubt that our friend and lawyer Runes was at the center of this nightmare because he was one of the very few persons who knew where we hid our money and books.

It was a deeply painful realization, but at that point we did not have the time to react with the appropriate rage. We ran out of the office and up the two flights of stairs to the disco, intent on grabbing our expensive sound equipment, but there just wasn't enough time. Minutes later, Perlbinder, the city marshal, and yes, Richard Runes, arrived with a new court order revoking ours. We walked out of the club, for what would be the last time, with nothing. Passing the city marshal, Runes, and Perlbinder standing together on the sidewalk, I lurched at Runes and Perlbinder and screamed, *"You motherfuckers!"* I wanted to strangle them. They quickly backed away, like the cowards that they were, startled by my fury. I moved on because I had to. I didn't want to be arrested.

Perlbinder bought the property so he could develop it into what would later become a high-rise apartment building. While fighting our case in court, he leased the space, *rent free*, to the Policemen's Benevolent Association!

•

The aggregate power and strength of the four of us enabled us to open Sahara, buttressing and encouraging us to push through all the obstacles, but that unity was now gone. There were fractures in our relationships that had built up over the years and we could not regroup. Linda's mother had just died, and Linda isolated herself in mourning and medicated herself with drugs. Barbara stayed with her in their apartment out of a sense of love, loyalty, and mutual addiction. There was a wide distance between Michelle and me, too, caused by her drug use and recklessness. And I had already wanted to move on and they knew I was looking for a way out.

When our case finally went to court, based on the fact that we were not legally served a notice of eviction, the judge intimated to Runes and Perlbinder that he was going to rule in our favor. He suggested that it would be in their best interest to go into the hallway, while he took a short break, and negotiate a settlement with us.

We were excited, but once outside the courtroom, Runes and Perlbinder came down hard on us and said threateningly, "We have your books and we will turn them over to the IRS if you don't walk away from this lawsuit *right now*." Sahara was a cash business. Our accountant, who was experienced in the restaurant and nightclub business, *must* have accounted for our cash transactions, but with no way to contact him at that moment and the clock ticking while the judge was in recess, there was no way to be sure. We were frightened.

Perlbinder's weak offer to us was that he'd return everything from the club that was now in storage. We quickly weighed our options. The club had been closed for months now and to restart the business would have been difficult, if not impossible, especially considering our own splintered partnership and lack of funds. We figured we could at least get some money out of the sale of the inventory and equipment, I could get the art back and, with those resources, we could jump-start our lives again.

The judge waited in the courtroom for our agreement. We were beaten down, scared, young, and admittedly inexperienced. We fell for their ploy. They were blackmailing us but we simply couldn't afford any more legal battles. We decided that we had all had enough and agreed to walk away.

Following through with Perlbinder's offer, we went to the storage warehouse in Harlem, where our Sahara inventory, art, and equipment were supposedly held. Futilely, we looked through the few boxes scattered around the warehouse floor. Everything of worth had disappeared: the lights, the sound equipment, and the costly bottles of liquor were all gone. The most heartbreaking loss was my art, which was nowhere to be found.

We confronted the slovenly, unshaven warehouse owner, and asked him what had happened to our property. He looked us straight in our faces and, clearly lying, said, "I have no idea." We were devastated. There was nothing at that warehouse to salvage and nothing more we could do. We lost a lot more than our physical possessions that day. We lost whatever innocence was left to us. All that remained was bitterness and rage.

•

The loss of Sahara and the resentment that consumed me caused problems in my relationship with Beth. At various times in our lives, Beth and I have each confronted and fought our own personal demons, like most people do. However, our private battles were often soothed by our love for each other.

At that time, Beth was working for a theatrical and movie payroll service. She was partially shielded from her social anxiety because she worked alone on payroll, away from the other employees. But when the company wanted her to be more of a team player, to become part of the company family, it petrified her. She was paranoid that people were judging her and she was living with tremendous shame because she had such difficulty participating with other people in the company's activities, living up to her own potential, and taking on more responsibility. She was tortured, obsessed with her inadequacies, and talked about her anxiety, fear, and sense of failure constantly.

With the demise of Sahara, I needed her to step away from her own self-absorption to take care of me. I was consumed by my desire for revenge against Richard Runes who had so deeply betrayed us and struggled to financially and emotionally survive. Everyday felt as if I was trying to breathe underwater. I resented Beth's selfishness. One night I came right out and said, "You have to put your own issues on the back burner. My problems have to take precedence right now. I need your full attention because I'm drowning and you're not there for me." She listened intently and thankfully understood. She hadn't fully grasped how bad off I was until then; loving me and being inherently fair, she said she would take better care of me and she did.

She put my needs before her own as I did for her at other times in our relationship. That was the balance we were always able to strike because we had faith in each other's honesty and integrity. This is the best advice I can give to other couples—be lovers, be passionate, but above all be friends. Don't let ego or power plays obscure your love for each other. *Surrender* when the situation calls for it.

15

Bashert: Fate, Meant to Be

Isn't it strange how the most horrific and wonderful events that occur in your life can happen within mere days of each other? In late November 1979, a month before Sahara closed, I received a phone call at the club from my old friend, the artist David Boyce. He had moved into his now ex-boyfriend Manuel's job as assistant director at the Sidney Janis Gallery after Manuel left. I hadn't spoken to David in ages.

He told me that the artist George Segal, the most famous representational American sculptor of the day and who was on the roster of the Sidney Janis Gallery, had been commissioned by the Mariposa Foundation and the Mildred Andrews Fund to create a sculpture to commemorate the 10th anniversary of the Stonewall riots and gay pride. Founded in 1978 by Bruce Voeller, with Karen DeCrow of the National Organization of Women and Aryeh Neier of the American Civil Liberties Union, to study human sexuality, Mariposa was an education, charity and research foundation. Voeller, who was a founder and former co–executive director of the National Gay Task Force (now called the National LGBTQ Task Force) where I had volunteered in the early 1970s, and who was someone I greatly admired, was spearheading the effort. Supported largely by private contributions, as well as public research grants, this commission was one of Mariposa's first projects. Voeller had proposed the idea to Peter Putnam, a wealthy arts patron and trustee of his mother's foundation, the Mildred Andrews Fund, which was dedicated to monumental public sculpture. Putnam agreed to commission and fund the sculpture. He had previously commissioned Segal's controversial monument to the students slain at Kent State.

The charge for a "homosexual liberation monument" to be placed in Christopher Park at Sheridan Square, across from the Stonewall Inn in Greenwich Village, stipulated only that the work "had to be loving and caring and show the affection that is the hallmark of gay people. And, it would have to equally represent men and women."

George Segal was famous for creating real-life tableaux by casting life-size figures in plaster within the environments they inhabited. Each sculpture told significant stories of humanity experiencing the joys and travails of life: the impoverished seeking a meal on a soup line, a man crossing the street, a bus driver at work. Segal's work was in more than sixty-five public collections, and he had been the subject of several major museum retrospectives.

He became known for being part of the Pop art movement, a group of artists who incorporated commonplace objects like road signs, comic strips, or soup cans into their art as subject matter. His style was distinct from Pop art, however, in that his work closely related to personal experience and human values. The sculpture would be permanently installed as a gift to New York City and was to be called *Gay Liberation*. George Segal asked David to help him find models, so David reached out to me.

David had already asked a mutual friend of ours to participate, a well-known art historian at a prestigious university, from the days when we all hung out together at David and Manuel's loft. She was hesitant about posing because she feared being "outed" to her parents. I told him about my relationship with Beth. I said if George Segal truly wanted to capture a special relationship between two women, Beth should be the one to pose with me. He agreed.

I was excited at the thought of the monumental impact this sculpture would have for gay people everywhere, not to mention that Beth and I would now be immortalized in a public sculpture permanently installed in New York City. It signified everything that mattered to me—art, our love, and visibility—and would positively impact the world's understanding and acceptance of homosexuality.

•

A few weeks after David's phone call, Beth and I were sitting in George Segal's studio, a converted chicken barn on his farm in South Brunswick, New Jersey, where his family had lived and raised chickens since the 1950s.

We were in awe of the sculptures arranged around the studio. Some were life-size statues of ordinary people in white plaster posed in different positions and settings, and others were just heads cast in plaster and painted in bold primary colors hanging on the white walls. It was kind of eerie, like a fun house filled with ghosts and goblins.

George took us outside to a long park bench where the sculpture would eventually come to life. We discussed what the sculpture would look like and posed in various seated positions on the bench while Segal took countless photographs. We encouraged George to show the intimacy that existed between us and to not avoid the sexual component of lesbian relationships out of a sense of propriety. We asked him not to camouflage us to the extent that observers might misinterpret us to be "just friends." When we were finished, George and his wife, Helen, treated us to a Chinese dinner at a local restaurant.

On our second trip to the studio, George knew the exact pose he wanted. The sculpture would depict a life-size male couple standing a few feet away from a female couple sitting together on a park bench. One of the men holds the shoulder of his friend. One of the women touches the thigh of her partner as they gaze into each other's eyes.

In a process that George pioneered, he used moistened plaster bandages (gauze strips designed for making orthopedic casts) as a medium and wrapped us in the bandages until they hardened—first our legs, then our midsections, and finally our heads. Straws were inserted in our noses so we could breathe. The sections were then cut off of us and put back together to form a hollow cast that

FIG. 28. Beth and me posing for the *Gay Liberation* sculpture outside George Segal's studio, a former chicken coop in New Brunswick, New Jersey. Photo credit: George Segal.

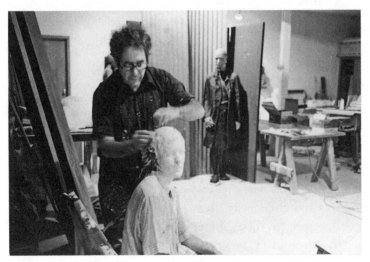

FIG. 29. George Segal casting Beth for the *Gay Liberation* sculpture; she felt claustrophobic when he covered her face with plaster whereas I felt a calm come over me and fell asleep inside the cast.

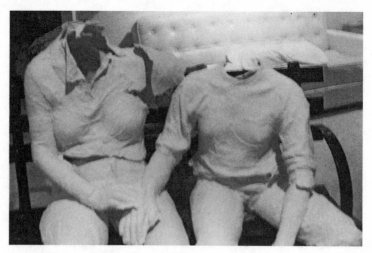

FIG. 30. Partially finished cast in Segal's studio.

would then be cast in bronze and, finally, painted white to resemble the original plaster.

After he was done plastering us, we left our cutout selves on the park bench in his studio and, once again, joined Helen for dinner. Then George drove us to the station to catch the train back to New York.

•

As exciting and revolutionary as the idea was for the *Gay Liberation* sculpture, it would take almost *thirteen years* for it to be installed in Christopher Park. Historical obstacles and prejudices presented themselves. After the war in Vietnam finally ended in 1975, after years of massive protests, women, African Americans, gays and lesbians, and other marginalized people continued their fight for equality and made major advances. But there was a backlash.

Threatened by these minorities, a New Right emerged, defending conservatism and traditional family values: Phyllis Schlafly taking on antiabortion and feminism and Anita Bryant and others on the warpath against gay and lesbian rights. When the AIDS plague took hold in the United States in 1980, the LGBTQ civil rights struggle faced further hostility led by figures like Reverend Jerry Falwell, whose "Moral Majority" inveighed against giving rights to gay people. As the antigay reaction gained steam across America with the election of Moral Majority ally Ronald Reagan, activists found their demands for attention for the growing medical crisis ignored. The march for LGBTQ civil rights, which had ground to a halt, was reactivated in 1987, when activists, frustrated by the government's inaction as they witnessed their relatives', friends', and lovers' bodies piling up, founded the AIDS Coalition to Unleash Power, or ACT UP, in New York City.

But this fervent conservatism and return to "family values" continued to echo in the controversy surrounding the *Gay Liberation* sculpture. The very first article to announce the sculpture was published in the *New York Times* on July 21, 1979.[1] In that piece, George Segal said the following: "Although I am not homosexual, I've lived in the art world for many years and I'm extremely sympathetic to the problems that gay people have. They are human beings, first. I couldn't refuse to do it."

The article also mentioned that to go forward, the sculpture required the approval of the Department of Parks, the local Community Board 2, and the city's Art Commission. This article became the kindling that started the fiery battle between those in favor of the sculpture and those who opposed it. In another article in the *New York Times* in August of 1980,[2] the various disputes were delineated. Some Greenwich Village residents argued that it was not the homosexual subject matter that was the issue but that it should not be located in Christopher Park. Others were just brazenly homophobic.

Some homosexuals complained that the proposed sculpture was not inclusive *enough*, in that it did not include a black or a Latin person. Some complained that the sculptor was not gay. Other gay people felt the sculpture was frivolous, actually trivializing the gay struggle.[3] The *Times* article also cited an unnamed gay activist who was distributing petitions "protesting that the figures in the sculpture are 'grotesque stereotypes offensive to all in the community.'"[4]

It was Bruce Voeller, George Segal, and a large contingent of national gay leaders, politicians, artists, writers and historians who deserved the credit and honor for fighting this long battle to install

Gay Liberation in Christopher Park. I played a very minor role in the effort except for the one night on September 8, 1980 when arguments for and against the sculpture came to a head at a volatile, jam-packed public hearing held at St. Vincent's Hospital in Greenwich Village. David reacted to the brewing battle and the upsetting quotation in the *New York Times* article calling us "grotesque stereotypes" by suggesting that we make T-shirts with the words "grotesque stereotypes" emblazoned across the front to wear to the hearing so that when the audience saw us, the irony would be apparent.

Sitting in that meeting was more painful than preparing for it. The four of us—Beth and I and the two male models—stood in front of a crowd of over 200 people, wearing our T-shirts. Some of the comments made were punctuated by obscenities and vitriol: "The statues are obscene . . . it's a piece of blatant exhibitionism . . . [it will] spread homosexuality among our youngsters . . . it's antihuman and means a gay takeover . . . it would become a pornographic shrine for them [gay people]." By the time it was my turn to speak, I was deeply offended. I approached the microphone and addressed the audience:

> We are "the grotesques stereotypes offensive to all in our
> community," referred to in the recent *New York Times* article.
> [The audience, seeing the humor, erupted into loud applause.]
> I'm so tired of listening to this kind of rhetoric, be it from gays
> or straights. It hurts me. It undermines who I am and who
> I choose to love. Stop it already. It's unfair and it's inhumane.
>
> Some have suggested placing a plaque in the park, instead of
> the sculpture, to commemorate the Stonewall uprising, but the
> problem is that few would see it, let alone read it. Visibility is
> the issue. Why not do what's most effective?
>
> This is not meant to be an explicit representation of Stone-
> wall. It is much broader than that—it represents gay liberation
> by openly showing our love for one another in a visual medium.
> There is no stronger statement than that in our quest for libera-
> tion. The bottom line in our struggle has always been the issue

of visibility. We must acknowledge this and we need your help—all of you—gay and straight. Must we really continue throwing bottles and screaming to prove we exist?

I wonder, with all due respect, to those of you attending this hearing tonight, if these were two heterosexual couples instead of homosexual couples, who modeled for this sculpture which celebrates love and respect between people, would there be such a brouhaha, such antagonism as we've seen in reaction to this piece? Or, instead, would we all be sitting here tonight celebrating the fact that the village has now become the recipient of a major sculpture by George Segal, a preeminent contemporary artist celebrated throughout the world?

16

After the Desert

The closing of Sahara was a gut wrenching punch to all of us. But having no income, I needed to find a job fast. I ended up driving a limousine when there were few, if any, other women doing that at the time. Al, a former bouncer at Sahara, owned a limousine company, which is how I got the job. Luckily for me, New York's transit system was on strike and Al needed more drivers. Al ran his limousine service out of his apartment in a high-rise building on York Avenue on the Upper East Side. A disco ball hung from the middle of the ceiling in the sparse living room that also served as his office. It threw speckled spots on Al's desk, chair, and the single couch that I and the other three drivers shared while we waited to be dispatched.

Flashbacks of my time with Joe and Tommy came to mind as I watched the guys yell out of the seventh-floor window at women they were ogling on the street below. With their heads hanging out of the window, one guy screamed, "Hey, baby! Look up here."

"Come up and join us," another yelled.

It was ridiculous, but they would not stop. I marveled at how men viewed harassing women as a pastime. After I'd had enough, I'd say, "Al, can't you *please* get your monkeys to stop howling?" But nothing discouraged them.

The guys did teach me how to "bang," though, which meant picking up unscheduled fares on the way back to the office after a booked fare was over. That way you could pocket the extra cash and

Al would be none the wiser. During the transportation strike, we were all "banging" like crazy, and I was finally making money again.

One night in early 1980, a few months after the club had closed, I arrived home totally exhausted from a difficult, long day of driving around the city. In my navy-blue pantsuit and white shirt, with my chauffeur's hat still on my head, I slumped down next to Beth on the couch, depressed and totally withered by self-pity and self-contempt. I was humiliated by the fact that, despite my high aspirations to make a living doing something artistic and creative by writing a screenplay (which I was still working on), I was now driving a limo for a living. I started thinking about the nightclub business again. My thoughts started to percolate with a new idea.

I knew from owning Sahara that a club could count on their Friday and Saturday nights being profitable, but bringing customers in on the other nights of the week was a challenge. Every club had a night or nights that were virtually empty and not profitable, yet the cost of keeping a club open remained the same. Suddenly, the proverbial lightbulb went off in my head. I had already amassed a large following from Sahara which had a stellar reputation that just grew more impressive with time. All that I was missing was a club. It dawned on me that I could bring my following to a slow night at another club and create a successful night for the owner and myself. It was a win-win situation. That's how the original idea of becoming a club promoter came to me.

Believe it or not, that concept of club promotion was nonexistent at the time. No one was doing it. If I could find a club owner willing to take a chance, I figured I could take over a night or two or three when they weren't doing good business on their own and run a weekly event that catered to my clientele, women. I told Beth about my idea and she loved it. The next day, I called Michelle, who was working for a friend's T shirt company at the time to make ends meet, and asked her if she wanted to do it with me. My one proviso was that she had to remain cocaine-free. She promised me that she was finished with cocaine and, as it turned out, she was.[1]

The concept was simple. The club owners ran the club and paid for all the overhead. We paid promotion costs and brought in the

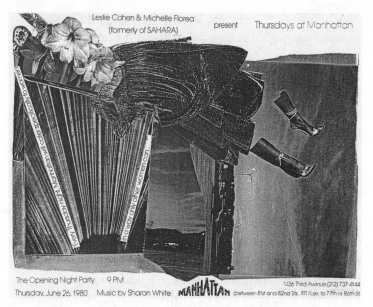

Leslie Cohen & Michelle Florea
(formerly of SAHARA)   present   Thursdays at Manhattan

The Opening Night Party   9 PM
Thursday, June 26, 1980   Music by Sharon White   **MANHATTAN**   1436 Third Avenue (212) 737-4144 (between 81st and 82nd Sts. IRT/Lex. to 77th or 86th St.)

FIG. 31. Invitation to Michelle's and my first club promotion, 1980; 700 women lined up on the street over the course of the night to get in. I love the artwork by my friend Miriam Hernandez.

clientele. We kept all or part of the admissions collected at the door and the owner kept the money from the bar. In June 1980, six months after Sahara closed, "Thursdays for Women" at Manhattan, a club on Third Avenue and East 81st Street, kicked off. Over the course of that opening night seven hundred women stood in line to get in. We were back—the fun, the women, the dancing, the exaltation, *and* we were making more money than we ever had before! This simple idea substantially changed the way the club business was conducted. It was so successful that we ended up promoting club nights for women for the next twenty years. Many other female promoters would follow our lead.

•

Getting involved with promoting provided Beth and me with not only financial resources but also the opportunity to work on her singing career, which I now managed. She quit her day job and began bartending at Manhattan to free up her time. Singing was a difficult transition into the public eye for her. At the beginning, she stood in front of me in the basement of our rented summerhouse in the Hamptons, trying to get up the nerve to sing again and struggling against her inhibitions. It was very difficult for her to be so vulnerable, even in front of me. She said, "I feel like I am undressing in front of strangers."

I coaxed her, "It's just you and me, no strangers. Just take a deep breath and give it a try."

Gradually, the wall of resistance crumbled and it became easier and easier. One day at the end of that summer, after weeks of practice, she said triumphantly, "I'm ready to put an act together and perform." It was obvious that music was her heart and soul and singing was the tool she used to let it out. For someone who had always been so socially uptight, to be able to open up and sing so beautifully was an enormous triumph and release. Her voice was a weapon she could use to fight her demons.

We began to search for original material that was vocally suitable for her to sing, hire musicians and musical directors, and book clubs, rehearsal times, and studio space. At first, with her new stage name "Beth Slade," she started performing rock 'n' roll material in clubs around the city, but then, realizing she was not a belter, she switched to the standards, which were much more suited to her laid-back, jazzy voice. She pushed herself, allowing herself to do things onstage that she could never do in real life. She could emote, be sexual, flirt, and entertain. The stage provided her with a protective barrier that shielded her from direct contact with the audience. Blinded by the stage lights, she only saw black. Removed and at a safe distance from the onlookers, she could take flight.

The more she sang, the more comfortable she became onstage. She started to perform in clubs around the city. Kay's friend Bill Barnes, the then well-known talent agent for Al Pacino and Raquel Welch, came to see Beth perform at one of her shows. After the show, Bill told Beth that he was very taken with her performance and was interested in representing her. Soon after, Bill booked her

On the image:

Beth Slade

Saturday, October 6th, 1984 • 11 p.m. (1 show)
Eric • 1700 Second Ave. (at 88th St.) • 534-8500 (Reservations Suggested)

FIG. 32. Invitation to Beth's performance at Eric's, 1984; I was so nervous for her. To lessen my anxiety, she let me perform her whole show in front of her while she sat on our living room couch. Photo credit: Leslie Cohen.

for a three-month engagement at the largest nightclub in Tokyo, the Mikado. She was hired as the star of an extravagant, Vegas-type show. The Mikado seated one thousand people. The gig entailed doing two shows a night, six nights a week. There would be multiple costume changes, assisted by her own dresser, a twenty-five-piece orchestra, and twenty dancers to accompany her.

Beth accepted the gig, as long as I came with her. I left the club we were promoting in New York City in Michelle's hands, and, in 1985, Beth and I went to Japan. I knew she needed to prove to herself that she could do it, even if it was not the kind of show that she would have ever imagined herself performing in. It was all Vegas glitz and glam, elaborate scenery and costumes, very different from the kind of singer that Beth was. She had to emote loudly over the large orchestra and the audience drinking and conversing, which was not conducive to her style; she was a crooner—emotive, sultry, and bluesy. Yet, she excelled.

They had her wearing sparkling, sequin-covered, skintight, floor-length dresses, large feathered headgear, and a ton of makeup. She looked like a drag queen. The enormous room had a waterfall against the far wall and tables and banquettes set up in a semi-circle facing the stage. She was playing to Japanese businessmen and the hostesses that coddled them.

After three months, we came back to New York from Japan. Bill already had plans to book Beth into Atlantic City or Las Vegas as an opening act for either George Burns or Buddy Hackett, stars from our and our parents' generation who were still popular. It was all very exciting but not what she wanted. After meeting with Bill, Beth said to me, "I don't think I really want to do this. This is going to take me away from you. I'm going to have to be on the road and live out of a suitcase. I don't want that life. I'm not a Vegas type of act. It's not the kind of singer I am. Besides, I do not want to be without you every day."

I said, "But you've worked so hard at this and you're on the verge of real success . . . are you sure?"

She answered, "Yes. It's okay. I see I could be successful if I want it, and that's all I need to know. I don't want to be living on the road without you. I will not be happy."

Even though we had put a lot of time and money into developing her career, I wasn't surprised or angry. Besides, I felt the same way. We realized that a life on the road, often separate from each other, would not work for us. It was not an easy decision, but it made sense.

FIG. 33. Beth and her costume dresser at the Mikado nightclub in Tokyo, Japan, 1985.

Understanding that her decision was final, I asked her, "So, my love, what do you want to do now?"

She said, "There are many things in my life that I get excited about. I think I should go back to school. I've always wanted to be a psychotherapist and take people through their inner journey. Helping other people would make me happy." And so, after a couple of years of hard work, Beth received her master of social work degree, became a psychotherapist, and opened her own practice in New York.

•

Throughout the 1980s and 1990s, Michelle and I promoted many club nights for women in New York City and in the Hamptons on the eastern end of Long Island. Eventually, however, promoting had become a financial roller coaster ride. As feminism progressed, more and more women sought to create their own businesses. Naturally, there was now growing competition from other women who jumped on the nightclub promotion bandwagon.

You're in and then you're out. Like Robert said, "Style gets used up." There was always another new club or night that ended your run. Women would want to go to the newest happening place because it was fresh and up to the minute. Then your crowd would thin out. Once that occurred, your business was doomed and you would slowly watch it die. The club business had little to do with loyalty. Your only salvation would be to find another, cooler place to promote and hopefully on a good night, like a Friday or Saturday, as opposed to say a Monday night when few women would go out. It became more and more difficult to find the right dance club on the right nights. But if you did, you were back in the game. It was a vicious cycle. I always got a kick out of women who said that there were enough women to go around to support more than one promoter on the same night, but that was usually not true. The women's market was a very limited market.

It became exhausting not knowing where my next dollar was coming from, especially as I approached my forties. It just did not make sense to continue promoting club nights for women as my sole means of making a living. I became determined to find another direction. Over the following years, I was all over the place. I

FIG. 34. Beth, Michelle, and me at the first club Michelle and I promoted in East Hampton, Long Island, 1985. Our Hampton promotions were very successful and so much fun.

wrestled with deciding what other profession would fit me. Could I be a painter, a writer, a filmmaker? Should I sell real estate or go to business school? The possibility of getting back into the art world didn't seem viable at my age, especially with the four-year gap in my resume from when I owned Sahara. I had already been my own boss, so working for someone else would be a real challenge. I knew what it was like to have money and I didn't want to go without it again. All the time I promoted I agonized about this, to the point of exhausting not only myself but everyone around me who tried to help. I finally said to myself, *Just choose something and do it.*

Beth's mother was the one who suggested that I go to law school. I wanted a good income, security, and a profession where I could age gracefully and not become an anachronism. It was a very logical decision to apply to law school. In 1989, at the age of forty-two, I was accepted into New York University School of Law, one of the top ten law schools in the country, and I decided to enroll. I was the oldest student in my class.

•

On June 22, 1992, soon after I graduated from law school and three weeks before Beth and I moved to Miami where I had been hired

FIG. 35. The sculpture *Gay Liberation* in Christopher Park, Greenwich Village, New York.

by a large law firm, we received a telephone call from David. He told us that *finally*, after thirteen years, the *Gay Liberation* sculpture was going to be unveiled by Mayor David N. Dinkins and Park Commissioner Betsy Gotbaum in Christopher Park across from the Stonewall Inn. Hallelujah!

The next day, Beth, my mother, and I went to the unveiling. When we arrived at the park, it was filled with politicians, civic leaders, and the media. George Segal was there and we warmly embraced, happy to reconnect and celebrate our long-awaited victory. And then, from across the park, I saw a familiar face.

Suddenly, I realized it was the guy I had picked up on the subway so many years before when I lived with Michelle! He was now one of Mayor Dinkins's top aides. I pointed him out to Beth, who knew the story and, even though I resisted, insisted I go over and remind him of who I was.

I awkwardly approached him and said, "Hi, I'm Leslie. I don't know if you remember me but we had a rendezvous on the subway many years ago." He looked at me for a moment and then lit up. "Of course, I remember you," he said as he pulled me to him and hugged me. Then, when I told him we were the models for the sculpture, he couldn't believe it and eagerly introduced us to the mayor when he arrived at the park.

There were numerous speeches given by city officials, including Mayor Dinkins and Councilwoman Ruth Messinger. Afterward, we were photographed and interviewed with and without the mayor by newspapers, magazines, television, and radio. My mother, who loved the limelight (it must be hereditary), kept bobbing her head up and down between Beth and me, exclaiming: "I am the *Mother!* I am the *Mother!*"

Gay Liberation was finally unveiled in the park for the world to see. It was an incredible send-off for Beth and me as we embarked on the next chapter of our lives in Miami. We knew that we would now forever remain a part of New York City as a symbol of the freedom to love.

•

I had been hired straight out of law school by a large, highly respected, and conservative law firm in Miami. We initially rented an apartment in Miami Beach on Collins Avenue on the ocean. What a change from our tiny, 560-square-foot, ground-floor, apartment in Manhattan, where we had to lie on our backs on our bed in order to catch a glimpse of a small patch of sky from our window. Even though we had a small backyard, considered a real luxury in New York City, when we went outside to enjoy some fresh air we usually came back into the apartment with tufts of lint that blew out of the vent from the laundry room next door clinging to

FIG. 36. Beth and me at the unveiling of *Gay Liberation*, 1992; an incredible day after waiting for so many years. Photo credit: Jonathan Kuhn.

our hair, and clothes smelling of laundry detergent. That was one of the main reasons we were ready to leave New York. We had had enough of living in a dark, viewless, cramped space and longed for clean air and openness.

Our two-bedroom apartment in Miami Beach faced the Intracoastal Waterway, where we could see rowers from the University of Miami glide past our windows in the early morning sun that reflected like starbursts off the water. At sunset, we would lie on our bed and now see the shadows of palm trees dancing seductively across our walls in a bedroom turned iridescent orange from the sunset. And we had the ocean in our backyard.

For the first few years after we moved, I worked at law firms to help me pay off my school loans and learn the ropes. I knew I would not last there for long. The first law firm I joined did not know I was gay. Women had to wear skirts or dresses, something I hadn't done in years. In the mornings, I would struggle to put on my panty hose, bra, and dirndl skirt and matching jacket. I hated it. Beth would look at me and sympathetically laugh, saying I reminded her of Robin Williams in the movie *Mrs. Doubtfire*, except Robin walked better in pumps than I did!

The second law firm was a much better professional fit for me than the first firm. At least there I could wear pants and be out as a lesbian. But I still didn't fit the firm culture. As an older adult, my priorities were different. The young associates were working their way up the partnership ladder. They still had something to prove to themselves. I was forty-five years old and had already attained success in other fields. My goal was financial freedom so I could be with Beth and do whatever I wanted with my time. And I needed to be my own boss.

We bought our first home in 1995, and in 1996, I opened my own practice. I remained a sole practitioner in private practice for another ten years until we were able to retire. My practice focused on bankruptcy, personal injury, and medical malpractice law and I did quite well. Did I love it? No, but law provided me with the stability and financial resources that I had hoped for. During those years, Beth worked as a psychotherapist with various groups, including psychotic elders and pediatric AIDS children and their families. Her last job was as a trust counselor in the Miami-Dade County Public Schools, a kind of hybrid job that required her skills as a psychotherapist and teacher.

In 2005, bankruptcy laws changed and my practice was threatened as a result. At the same time, Beth was feeling enormous stress in her job at a high school in the inner city. She was highly sensitive to criticism from her very difficult principal and the students, who were aggressive, hostile, and continually acting out. I was unable to help her. I was so stressed out from work and self-absorbed by my own problems that by the end of the day I had nothing left to give her. I just wanted to be left alone. Our relationship was under enormous strain and was fraying from lack of care.

One night, during a moment of clarity, I looked closely at her. She didn't feel well. Her eyes had dark circles under them and her skin had an unhealthy gray tinge. I became very concerned.

The stress was killing us both, but the realization that her health was suffering and that I could lose her if we didn't make a drastic change in our lives hit me like a rockslide. It forced me to fundamentally examine and reaffirm what really mattered to me, to look at what our life had become and what it would be like without Beth. The loss would be unbearable. That's when we sat down and decided that we had to find a way to reunite and live as stress-free a life as possible. I worked the financial numbers over and over again to figure out how we could retire. It didn't matter anymore where or how we lived. All we wanted was to be healthy and together. If all we could afford was a studio somewhere in the middle of nowhere, that was what we were going to do.

Fortunately, our home had appreciated considerably. In late 2006, we sold the house and retired. We were fifty-eight years old. For so long, we had wanted enough money to not have to answer to anyone, to not have to worry anymore about paying our bills, to have what we called "fuck you" money. When we had finally achieved our dream—become masters of our own lives to play with our creative dreams and be together—we were beyond jubilant.

•

Beth has surely been the blessing in my life but, naturally, it hasn't always been good times. Life is not simple like that and happiness is sometimes elusive. We have both endured enormous losses together—the deaths of my mother and both of Beth's parents, my aunts, uncles, my brother Michael, my friends Kay, Helene, John, David, Robert, and so many more.

Throughout our more than forty-five years together as a couple, and fifty-six plus years since we first met in college, of course there have been some very rough patches—times when our own depression from the shadows of our pasts or the realities of our present became overbearing. Don't most, if not all of us, suffer at times from a general malaise, a pervasive listlessness, "the subjective condition that some call ontological anxiety or existential dread" which is "basically the fear of being, a feeling that there is no meaning to life"?[2] Beth and I certainly have each suffered in that way, in

FIG. 37. Beth and me in our apartment in Miami, 2016; this is what life is like for us now. Photo credit: Donna Victor.

that private hell, and that state of mind is never easy to handle for oneself, let alone in a relationship.

But love and commitment create a force field of sorts to combat that existential dread. You cannot hide from the harsh realities and precariousness of life, the severity of which is often determined randomly or accentuated by where or when you were born or the color of your skin; but perhaps at times, if you are very lucky and you find love, you can counteract those things. Certainly, no one should be denied that chance because of the gender of the person they choose to love.

Postscript

Sahara's success represented a paradigm shift, a pivotal moment in history when women began to take control of their lives, insistent on being seen and heard. Lesbians and homosexuals also began to break the strictures that bound them. Sahara existed at the intersection of those two vectors of change and gave both lesbians and straight women a place of sanctuary at that moment in time.

I want to believe that Sahara made a significant contribution to the ongoing conversation of gender and gay and lesbian equality, which is as critical now as it was in the late 1960s and 1970s, especially with the current battle for transgender rights and the threat to established gay and lesbian rights such as marriage. Many women have told me and my partners that Sahara was a game changer for them personally.

If Sahara was so important to lesbians and feminists at the time, why, you might ask, don't more people know about it? I've asked myself the same question. Perhaps the question should really be what and who determines the value of human experience. Does gender discrimination establish that women's experiences are less valued than men's (gay men included), or is it women's lack of bravado and self-aggrandizement that is to blame? I suppose it's both. What I do know for sure is that we must tell our stories if we want to be counted.

What you hold in your hands is a story that has never been documented in full. Sahara is not included in any widely read accounts of lesbian, gay, or feminist history, which is an omission that I wanted to correct, and one of the reasons I wrote this book.

The four of us—me, Michelle, Barbara, and Linda—succeeded against *all odds*. But, like so much of women's history and accomplishments, if I didn't resurrect our moment in lesbian and feminist history, it would disappear into the quagmire of time as if it had never existed.

But it *did*.

The experience we had at Sahara and the many nights I shared with women in the clubs Michelle and I promoted over the next twenty years fills me with an enormous sense of gratitude. There was nothing else, workwise, that ever made me happier or was more fulfilling. Thank you to all the women with whom we shared the rapture.

•

Since the unveiling of the sculpture in 1992, Beth and I have stood before *Gay Liberation* many times, staring at our doppelganger selves, the reflection of our love for each other and our pride in the LGBTQ+ community.

This is the other reason I wrote this book. Perhaps, one day, when Beth and I are long gone, your children, or grandchildren—straight, lesbian, gay, transgender, or whatever—may find themselves standing before the *Gay Liberation* sculpture in Christopher Park in the West Village of New York City. It will mean so much to us if whoever is looking and, possibly, wondering who those two women sitting on the bench were, knows that we were two women who spent a lifetime together and were very much in love, and that that possibility belongs to them, too.

Endpiece. Beth and me, the *Gay Liberation* sculpture by George Segal in Christopher Park, Greenwich Village, New York.

The human being is capable of an infinity of gestures and attitudes. My biggest job is to select and freeze the gestures that are most telling. . . . To capture a subject's gravity and dignity . . . I'm dependent on the sitter's human spirit to achieve total effectiveness.

—George Segal, quoted in *Pop Art*, Lucy Lippard, 1966

Gay Liberation Timeline

June 1979	Sculpture was announced.
September 1980	Backlash about the sculpture began.
June 1992	Sculpture unveiled in Christopher Park.
June 28, 1999	Christopher Park, the Stonewall Inn, and its neighboring streets became a National Register of Historic Places site. Out of 70,000 such listings, this would be the first to be dedicated to LGBTQ+ accomplishments.
June 23, 2015	The Stonewall Inn became a New York City landmark, making it the first LGBTQ+ city landmark.
June 24, 2016	President Barack Obama officially designated the Stonewall Inn, the *Gay Liberation* sculpture, and the surrounding area *The Stonewall National Monument*, making it the United States's first national monument designated an LGBTQ+ historic site.

Acknowledgments

I first have to start my list by thanking my dear friends and partners who created Sahara with me: Linda Goldfarb, Barbara Russo, and Michelle Florea. Without them Sahara would never have become a reality.

I first started this memoir when I took a memoir writing class at Duke University in 2008, after Beth and I had retired and briefly moved to Durham, North Carolina. By 2011, after moving back to Miami in 2009, I had completed twenty-three pages. Frustrated by a two-year-long attempt by a producer and director to make a documentary on our love story, the sculpture, and Sahara that unfortunately never completely got off the ground, I reached out to Adrienne Rubin, my college roommate, about connecting me to her childhood friend, Andy Port, an editor at the *New York Times* whom I had met many years before. I wanted to see if she knew anyone who might be interested in writing an article on our story. I offhandedly mentioned that I had started writing a memoir and she asked to see it, although I initially protested because I did not consider myself a writer and was frightened that I would embarrass myself. But, to my total surprise, she loved it and gave it to her editor in chief, Sally Singer, to read. Sally also loved the piece and decided to publish it, with Andy's editorial guidance, in the *New York Times*'s *T Magazine* as a full-length article in October 2011.

So, the first people I want to thank are the original producer and director of the unreleased documentary, my friends Bianca Lanza and Ricardo Bruno, for being so enthusiastic about our story and trying so hard to produce it. I thank Adrienne Rubin for our many years of friendship and for always having my back, and I especially want to thank Andy Port for her editorial brilliance and never-ending support and advice throughout all the years that followed before this book was complete. This book would not have happened without her encouragement.

I am deeply grateful to my friends who have nurtured and loved me along this long and winding road. There are too many to mention here but there are some people I would like to name specifically. Thank you to all who have read my seemingly endless versions of rewrites, offered much needed advice, and encouraged me to keep going: Carolee Shepard, Roberta Quinn, Ellen Haimoff, Michelle Florea, Barbara Russo, Howard Schor, Dana Ardi, David Gale, Mumball Lane, Dyan Grey, Alix Kucker, Ellen Bogen, Joy Suskin, the late David Boyce, Bonnie Levy, Heather Brighton, Marcie Imberman, Lisa Sharkey, Joanna Clarke, Jamie Robinson and especially Erin McHugh and Brian Kantz. My dear friend Elaine Gold is owed many gold medals for her patience in reading my multiple versions of the manuscript and for her devotion as a subsequent producer on our unfinished documentary. I am humbled by the generous spirit and love of all my friends.

I am indebted to the many people at Rutgers University Press who worked to make this book available. I am especially grateful to the editorial director, Kimberly Guinta, who decided to acquire this book in the first place and worked diligently to perfect it, and the copyeditor Katherine Woodrow and production supervisor, Deborah Masi of Westchester Publishing Services, who scoured it clean. Thank you Jeremy Grainger, Courtney Brach, Jasper Chang, Savannah Porcelli, Brice Hammack, and anyone else I might have missed, for your hard work and commitment. Without you this book would not be.

My most precious thanks and gratitude go out to two people in particular. When I was wondering how I could improve my manuscript, I reached out to Kim Green, a writing coach and editor. She devoted herself tirelessly to a comprehensive edit and restructuring of the manuscript. Thank you so much for your editorial and creative input that is present throughout this book.

Without your unwavering devotion to this project, my vision for this book would have not been fulfilled. Thank you, Kim, for all you did to make this a reality.

And finally, to my wife, best friend, and lifelong love, Beth Suskin. She never wavered in her support of me. She read so many versions of rewrites that we lost count. She held me up when I faltered, advised me throughout everything, and encouraged me to continue during the many years of stop-and-go progress. I love you from the depths of my heart and soul.

•

All images in this book are from my personal collection except when otherwise noted.

Notes

Chapter 4 Awakening

1. Barry Adam, *The Rise of a Gay and Lesbian Movement* (Boston: Twayne/G. K. Hall & Co., 1987).

2. Nicholas Edsall, *Toward Stonewall: Homosexuality and Society in the Modern Western World* (Charlottesville: University of Virginia Press, 2003).

3. Martin Duberman, *Stonewall: The Definitive Story of the LGBTQ Rights Uprising That Changed America* (New York: Penguin Books, 1993).

4. "An adult convicted of the crime of having sex with another consent-ing adult in the privacy of his or her home could get anywhere from a light fine to five, ten, or twenty years—or even life—in prison. In 1971, twenty states had 'sex psychopath' laws that permitted the detaining of homosexuals for that reason alone. In Pennsylvania and California sex offenders could be committed to a psychiatric institution for life, and [in] seven states they could be castrated." David Carter, *Stonewall: The Riots That Sparked the Gay Revolution* (New York: St. Martin's Press, 2004).

5. Meredith Tax, Jo Freeman, Ellen Willis, Suzie Olah, Pamela Kearon, Carol Hanisch, Bonnie Kreps, Barbara Mehrhof, Irene Peslikis, and Kate Millet, *Notes from the Second Year: Women's Liberation: Major Writings of the Radical Feminists*, January 1, 1970.

6. "In the late nineteen-sixties, [Shulamith] Firestone and a small cadre of her 'sisters' were at the radical edge of a movement that profoundly changed American society. At the time, women held almost no major elected positions, nearly every prestigious profession was a male

preserve, homemaking was women's highest calling, abortion was virtually illegal, and rape was a stigma to be borne in silence. . . . Firestone believed . . . 'The end goal of feminist revolution must be, unlike that of the first feminist movement, not just the elimination of male *privilege* but of the sex distinction itself: genital difference between human beings would no longer matter culturally.'" Susan Faludi, "Death of a Revolutionary," *New Yorker*, April 15, 2013, newyorker.com.

Chapter 5 Crawling out of Darkness

1. Radclyffe Hall, *The Well of Loneliness* (London, Jonathan Cape, 1928). A lesbian novel that follows the life of Stephen Gordon, a wealthy Englishwoman, whose "sexual inversion" is apparent from an early age.

Chapter 6 Acceptance

1. Until 1974, the American Psychiatric Association's Diagnostic and Statistical Manual of Mental Disorders (the DSM) listed same-sex desires as a mental disorder, leading psychiatrists and medical professionals across the country to treat these feelings as akin to a disease. The classification was also the basis for laws criminalizing queer intimacy.

Part II

1. © 1996. Used with permission of Chronicle Books LLC, San Francisco. See ChronicleBooks.com.

Chapter 9 Jagged, Dirty Thoughts

1. Alix Kucker, who within a very short time would become instrumental to our success as our political liaison and producer of fundraising events, reflected on the opening night experience:

The private opening night of Sahara, to this day, was probably the most spectacular party I ever attended. A lot of people there were faces the general public would know but most were not out yet. Beautiful, talented, accomplished doctors, lawyers, journalists, authors, politicians, artists, you name it, they were there and they were stunning.

2. In 1978, Sahara held a benefit for *Heresies*, a new feminist publication on art and politics, with special guest appearances by Rita Mae Brown, Sheila Jordon, Eve Merriam, and Adrienne Rich. The invitation included a statement I wrote about my philosophy of hanging art at Sahara:

> Leslie Cohen . . . felt that the traditional means of exhibiting art, i.e. gallery/museum, was experientially limiting. The space in which a contemporary piece is hung has taken on more and more importance in relation to the experience a viewer might have. Often one feels alienated viewing art within the conventional context of the "white cube" that is the gallery or museum. . . .
>
> By hanging art on the walls of Sahara, Leslie hoped to create a new context of spectator/art—one in which art played an active part in the social atmosphere of the club. Those who come to socialize are benefitted by exhibiting and viewing art in a space where the art becomes part of a real-life experience. Human drama interacts with art.
>
> To date the following artists have exhibited at Sahara: Harriet Korman, Helene Aylon, Miriam Hernandez, Ronnie Reder, Sarah Lewis, Dianora Niccolini, Nancy Spero, Mary Beth Edelson, Pat Lasch, Joan Snyder, Louise Fishman, Gloria Beckerman, Harmony Hammond, Su Friedrich, Jane Hoffer, Dotty Attie, Kate Millett, Trudy Rosen, and Nina Prantis.

Chapter 10 An Antidote to Boredom

1. In conjunction with the growing feminist movement of the early 1970s, the roles of butch and femme that developed in lesbian bars in the 1950s and 1960s were rejected by lesbian feminists, who considered the butch roles archaic imitations of masculine behavior. Lillian Faderman, *Odd*

Girls and Twilight Lovers: A History of Lesbian Life in Twentieth-Century America (New York: Columbia University Press, 1991).

Chapter 13 Lone Riders

1. Susan Faludi, "Death of a Revolutionary," *New Yorker*, April 15, 2013, newyorker.com, quoting Anselma Dell'Olio in a 1970 address titled "Divisiveness and Self-Destruction in the Women's Movement: A Letter of Resignation."

Chapter 14 Style Gets Used Up

1. Other members of the caucus included Sidney Abbott, Steve Severson, Don Clay, Barrett Brick, Roz Pulitzer, Bruce Voeller, Ginny Apuzzo, Dolores Alexander, Jean O'Leary, Eleanor Cooper, and Pat Moriarty.
2. Intro 384 Gay Civil Rights Bill. Originally introduced in 1971 by the New York City Council as Intro 475, the bill was finally passed in 1986. The bill amends the administrative code of New York City to ban discrimination on the basis of sexual orientation in housing, employment and public accommodations.
3. Sahara held a fundraiser to benefit the Dade County Defense Fund with appearances by singer Lana Cantrell and feminist activist Flo Kennedy.
4. Lucy Hughes-Hallett, *The Pike: Gabriele D'Annunzio: Poet, Seducer, and Preacher of War* (New York: Anchor Books, 2014).

Chapter 15 Bashert: Fate, Meant to Be

1. Grace Glueck, "Homosexual-Liberation Statue Is Planned for Sheridan Square," *New York Times*, July 21, 1979.
2. Edith Evans Asbury, "Sculpture Planned for 'Village' Brings Objections," *New York Times*, August 28, 1980.
3. Craig Rodwell, "Some Objections to the Segal Gay Liberation Statue," flyer, September 5, 1980. Craig Rodwell was the owner of the Oscar Wilde Memorial Bookshop at 15 Christopher Street.
4. Marie Haggberg, "Neighbors Clash at Hearing on Gay Statues," *Villager*, September 11, 1980, referring to a statement by gay activist Ed

Murphy: "These statues don't look like me or my black brother, or my Spanish brothers, and should therefore be replaced by a plaque."

Chapter 16   After the Desert

1. After Sahara closed Barbara and Linda mourned the loss of Sahara and Linda's mother until they could pull themselves together enough to make other plans. Barbara bartended to make ends meet. In 1982, she and Linda opened another club called Moonshadow which became a successful gay men's club. Eventually they split up and went their own ways. I have remained friends with all of my Sahara partners. Michelle and I are closer than ever.

2. Mihaly Csikszentmihalyi, *Flow: The Psychology of Optimal Experience* (New York: Harper Perennial Modern Classics, 2008).

About the Author

LESLIE COHEN is a freelance writer who currently lives in South Florida. She grew up in Queens, New York, and attended Buffalo State College and then Queens College in 1969, where she received her master's degree in art history. She worked at *Artforum* magazine and as the curator of the New York Cultural Center in Manhattan. In 1976, she and her partners opened the Sahara nightclub in New York City, a groundbreaking, elegant women's nightclub which hosted, at different times, Pat Benatar, Betty Friedan, Gloria Steinem, Bella Abzug, Carol Bellamy, Adrienne Rich, Patti Smith, and many others. She eventually became a nightclub promoter, and then went to New York University School of Law in 1989. Leslie is also, along with her wife, Beth, the model for the sculpture *Gay Liberation* by George Segal, which resides in Christopher Park in Greenwich Village, outside the Stonewall Inn. After years of controversy (it was created in 1979 to commemorate the Stonewall rebellion), it was finally unveiled in 1992, and has become an international icon for the LGBTQ+ community and part of the Stonewall National Monument, the United States's first national monument designated an LGBTQ+ historic site. She retired after many years at her own firm in Miami. In October 2011, her article on which this book is based, "Love in the Time of Stonewall," was published in the *New York Times*'s *T* magazine. Leslie and Beth have been together for forty-five years and live in Miami with their cat, Birdie.